John Pritchard is Bishop of Jarrow. He was Archdeacon of Canterbury and, before that, Warden of Cranmer Hall, Durham. He has served in parishes in Birmingham and Taunton and has been Diocesan Youth Officer for Bath and Wells diocese. Previous books by the author include *The Intercessions Handbook*, *The Second Intercessions Handbook*, *Beginning Again*, *Living the Gospel Stories Today*, *How to Pray* and *Living Easter through the Year*. He is married with two daughters.

HOW TO EXPLAIN
YOUR FAITH

John Pritchard

First published in Great Britain in 2006

Society for Promoting Christian Knowledge
36 Causton Street
London SW1P 4ST

British Library Cataloguing-in-Publication Data
A catalogue record for this book is available from the British Library

ISBN-13: 978–0–281–05708–5
ISBN-10: 0–281–05708–7

1 3 5 7 9 10 8 6 4 2

Typeset by Graphicraft Ltd., Hong Kong
Printed in Great Britain by Ashford Colour Press

Contents

Contents

Part Three
WHY GET INVOLVED?

A word at the beginning

I suppose I'm just naturally curious. All my life I've nagged away at questions of faith. Why do I believe this or that? Indeed *do* I believe those things or am I just accepting what I used to believe or what others told me? When I was a vicar and newcomers came into church and sat there, awkward and confused, mentally I was always sitting with them, seeing these strange antics through their puzzled eyes.

Always there have been questions. When I pray, what do I think I'm doing? How can I believe in God when the latest horror spreads across my TV screen? Why did God have it in for the Amalekites? Can you be cool and a Christian? Why is the Church sometimes so absurd? Questions, questions, questions.

But at least it keeps you on your toes. I've found myself going back to the root questions again and again to check out the answers and to reformulate my reasons for faith. And when it comes down to it, I've always found those reasons to believe outweighing the reasons to panic. (And yes, I've asked myself all the questions about my psychological needs as well.)

My hope is that this book will help Christians talk more confidently with their friends about the hope that is in them. I think we're often tongue-tied when it comes to explaining our faith. We hope no-one will ask us why we actually believe in God, or how a loving God can let such tragedies happen. We wince when the questions get too close. 'Hasn't science disproved religion?' 'Church-goers are a load of hypocrites!' 'All religions are the same, aren't they?' And so on. Here in this book are some of the approaches that have helped me in answering those challenges.

I also hope the book might fall into the hands of people who are at present outside a faith community, but are interested in how Christians and others answer hard questions. I hope these approaches might provoke further thought, or maybe even a conversation with some hapless Christian!

So here we are, with a book that says where I've got to this year. Next year I might write it differently. Indeed I hope I would, because a faith that's alive will keep on taking in new ideas and fresh information, and crunching it through the mental computer with all the other stuff I've accumulated through the years. Does it still make sense? Yes I believe it does. So on we go.

More people have helped me on this journey of enquiry than will ever know. I've listened to them, taken down their thoughts, pressed them to say more, pondered their wisdom. I've read incessantly, and sometimes struck seams of gold. (John V. Taylor comes to mind.) I've valued the sceptical friends and read the cynical journalists. I've sat in the darkness and wondered what to make of it all. But above all I've talked. To wise friends like David Day and Ruth Etchells and Judy Hirst. To old friends like Anne Dunning and Ernest Smith and Ron Dauben. To loving family like Wendy, Amanda and Nicola. But crucially to my father, God rest him, who taught me to think, who never stopped thinking himself, and who I probably grow more like every year. To him I dedicate this book with deep affection.

John Pritchard

Part One

WHY BOTHER?

1

Starting far enough back

What they say

- 'What's all the fuss about religion and spirituality? Life is life. You are what you are. You do your best and enjoy it. There's no need for this "other dimension" of religion.'
- 'Christians go on about a "spiritual journey" but that makes far too many assumptions. I'm not even sure there's a journey to go on.'
- 'Religious people usually give me answers before I've got questions. I don't know if I've got any questions anyway.'

```
* * * * * * * * * * * * * * * * * * * * * * * * * * * * * *
*                                                         *
*  Star quote                                             *
*                                                         *
*  The Church doesn't come into it. I just live my life as I believe  *
*  I should live it, and make my decisions and hope they're good  *
*  ones, and have respect for other people. That's it.    *
*              Londoner interviewed in a research project *
*                                                         *
* * * * * * * * * * * * * * * * * * * * * * * * * * * * * *
```

Key issue

Believers and non-believers seem to live in different worlds. Believers assume too much. They think that everyone is unconsciously asking profound questions that need a 'religious' answer. But believers are sometimes still stuck in tired, predictable language and frozen forms of religion. These inherited expressions of faith often lack any real power to communicate to generations not brought up on the Christian story or the Church's liturgies. Much religious language has died. Believers need to start further back.

The Church can sometimes seem like a horse-drawn wagon being pulled along on square wheels. It's incredibly hard work for the horses. As it happens, inside the wagon is a cargo of round wheels. After struggling along for some miles one of the men driving the wagon team says: 'Look, we've got round wheels in the back. Why don't we try those?' The result is ridicule from the rest of the crew. 'These wheels were good enough for our parents and grandparents; we're not going to sell our heritage down the river!' So they struggle on, with everyone getting more and more exhausted and frustrated.

If only believers had more imagination!

What you might say

All kinds of basic human experiences have the potential to point beyond themselves. When people fall in love, for example, that intensity of relationship seems to push at the doors of something even bigger, something that love is only part of. It's as if you're falling into something vast and overwhelming. Some people try to make out it's only a functional activity that's really about sex. The same people might say that a kiss is just the coming together of two pairs of lips for the mutual transmission of microbes and carbon dioxide! But most people, when they fall in love, know they're in much deeper emotional territory. And some people recognize the experience as a doorway to a far, forgotten land.

It's the same with experiences of wonder. They point beyond themselves. It could be a furious sky full of storm and power. It could be standing at dawn gazing at Annapurna as sunlight strikes the awesome peaks around you (my experience). It could be listening to Beethoven's Ninth or standing before Michelangelo's *Pietà*. Or the exhilarating experience of riding a motor-bike at high speed, or of running when every part of you is humming with life. A recent survey found that feelings of awe were attached by people to a range of other, less obvious things, such as maths, being at sea, castles, flying, cemeteries, battlefields. We're taken out of ourselves, inspired, literally *in-spirited*. Something beyond us seems to reach out and take hold of us.

Some of these experiences draw out of us a sense of gratitude. Feelings of full-blown thankfulness rise up within us before we have time to censor them. It could be having your finger clasped by the tiny hand of a new-born child. Or coming home after a long time away. Or watching dolphins leap out of the sea. It's as if we've been given a gift and we need to thank something or someone for it. Christians call that something or someone, God.

There are times when we find that we're looking inside ourselves and don't know the way around! Our internal geography is more complex than we realized. Perhaps we have a bit of space on a long train journey, or we have a big decision to make, or we're facing an emotional crisis, and one thought just leads to another. Soon we find we're getting lost in space – inner space – and we realize that there's as much to explore *inside* ourselves as there is to discover *outside* ourselves. And that makes us feel a little dizzy, or lonely, or maybe even a bit scared. And sometimes what we discover inside us isn't very pleasant, and that's quite unnerving. But as well as the dark material, what we also find inside the caverns and mountains within us is a huge spring of compassion and tenderness. Our response to the Asian tsunami on Boxing Day 2004 was a testimony to that deep mercy. Again, this natural human experience of soul-searching draws us on to a larger map. It suggests that beneath the surface in any of us lies a massive substratum of complexity, energy and imagination.

The experience of tragedy also takes us to deeper places and more stretching questions. It might be the loss of a relationship or of a loved one; a horrific natural disaster or planes flying into the World Trade Center. We might be facing our own emotional disaster or the unimaginable slaughter of 800,000 Tutsis in Rwanda. We might be staggered at the way the guards at Auschwitz listened to Mozart in the evening and turned on the gas ovens in the morning; or be unable to comprehend how a terrorist can smile as he blows himself up along with scores of innocent bystanders. All of this faces us with darkness of a profound order and we need some hefty thinking to cope with it (see chapter 10 on suffering). Religious faith doesn't lessen the darkness but it is at least well practised in struggling with the problem. The Christian faith has the darkest of all symbols at its very heart – the crucified God. Life is both glorious and tragic on the same canvas, and Christianity doesn't duck the ambiguity or run the other way.

All these experiences, of love and wonder, of gratitude and soul-searching and tragedy, are invitations to look deeper. They offer thresholds into a bigger world of imagination and faith. There's no compulsion to follow that path or to see these things as questions: the experiences can simply be seen as incidents and accidents in the chronology of that insignificant little animal *homo sapiens*. But for millions of people the invitation to look deeper is quite persuasive. Dag Hammarskjöld, the first Secretary General of the United Nations, wrote: 'I don't know who – or what – put the question. I don't know when it was put. I don't even remember answering. But at some moment I did answer "Yes" to Some-one – or Something – and from that hour I was certain that existence is meaningful and that therefore my life, in self-surrender, had a goal.'

The heart of the matter

These deep experiences seem to point to life on a bigger map, a map that might be the most accurate and useful one we can find for the journey we all have to make. For many people, this map is called 'faith'.

Quotes for the conversation

When the black teenager Stephen Lawrence was killed on the streets of South London, the woman who cradled him as he died murmured over and over again to him: '*You are loved, Stephen, you are loved.*'

It is love, not German philosophy, that is the true explanation of this world – whatever may be the explanation of the next.

Oscar Wilde in The Ideal Husband

There's something charming and enchanting about the human spirit, in spite of our great negativity and fantastical laziness and indifference. There's also this mysterious thing called love. We may be really crooked and awkward and corrupt, and we mess things up. But once we fall in love with somebody or an idea or an action, that love itself suddenly makes us see the world differently . . . It's amazing what people do when they fall in love. We've got so many things inside us as part of our make-up. I think what is just needed is for those wonder elements in us to be touched, those springs of regeneration to be awoken.

Ben Okri, novelist

My eyes are almost burned by what I see. The fruit, the colours, mesmerize me in a quiet rapture that spins through my head . . . I lift an orange into the flat, filthy palm of my hand and feel and smell and lick it. The colour orange, the colour, the colour, my God the colour orange. Before me is a feast of colour. I feel myself begin to dance, slowly, I am intoxicated by the colour. Such wonder, such absolute wonder in such insignificant fruit . . . I want to bow before it, loving that blazing, roaring orange colour . . . I cannot hold the ecstasy of the moment and its passionate intensity. I am filled with a sense of love.

Brian Keenan, recounting an experience during his long imprisonment in Lebanon

One thing, truly experienced, even once, is enough for a lifetime.

Rilke, Austrian poet

For the past 80 years I've started each day in the same way. It's not a mechanical routine but something essential to my daily life. I go to the piano and play two preludes and fugues by Bach. I can't think of doing otherwise. It's a sort of benediction on the house. But that's not its only meaning for me. It's a rediscovery of the world of which I have the joy of being a part. It fills me with the awareness of the wonder of life, with a feeling of the incredible marvel of being a human being.

Pablo Casals, cellist

In the film *Chariots of Fire*, Eric Liddell is asked what he will do with his life. He says: 'I know God made me for China. But he also made me fast. And when I run I *feel* his pleasure.'

Story

The message in the bottle

Once upon a time there was an island where everyone seemed very content. Indeed apart from a little fishing, no-one ever left the island or even thought of doing so. The school system was basically fine, people had jobs, and they'd developed their political and community life to a pretty high standard. In particular they prided themselves on their language; they reckoned they knew how to communicate.

Nevertheless, just under the surface was something it was hard to put your finger on. A faint but pervasive dis-ease, a sense that something was missing, just out of reach. It was like a snatch of a forgotten melody, a scent of roses, a song in the night. Occasionally there was a crack in the smooth surface of life on the island and an unnamed frustration shot through and disturbed the peace. But it was quickly covered over.

One day, down on the beach, a green bottle was discovered with a piece of paper inside. An islander picked it up and read the piece of paper. 'Help is coming,' it said. Strange. He'd never heard that kind of language before. No-one ever needed any help on this lovely island. Nevertheless he was intrigued; it touched some level of awareness in him, but he had no name for it. He buried the message in the sand and threw the bottle away.

A few weeks later the man was walking on the beach again and found another bottle. It too had a message inside it which said this time: 'Help will arrive soon; don't give up.' Now this was really odd – two bottles couldn't be an accident. He told a friend. They went down to the beach together and looked out to sea. Day after day they went, and occasionally they found a bottle with these odd messages: 'Help set off yesterday,' or 'Take heart, help is definitely on its way.'

It was weird. They didn't need any help, but these messages were saying something different. Word got around. People joined them on the beach, watching the waves to see if there were any bottles coming in. People particularly came down on Sunday mornings. Weeks would go by without any bottles and then two or three would arrive together.

Those who gathered down on the beach shared a growing curiosity and a sense of wonder that they'd never known before. This was language being used in a quite new way. It didn't explain itself or try to convince them. It was just there, but it had a kind of pull on them, stronger than their normal, predictable language. They were being addressed by someone they didn't know, about something they didn't know they needed. Apparently the world was much larger than they'd previously realized, more than their language could handle. And maybe their lives also were bigger than they'd realized and more interesting than their language could describe. They were linked with a larger world, perhaps even with a *main*land. Perhaps they could be led out of their small island existence (their I-land) where they knew about everything – except perhaps themselves, and whoever was sending the messages in the bottles.

So they continued to gather on the beach, looking for bottles, reading the messages, walking, wondering. Some got bored of waiting and decided not to believe the messages. Others talked quietly among themselves, looking out to sea now and again. Still others brought their friends down to the beach and had a simple meal together.

Then, one morning no different from any other, the people on the beach saw something that made the hairs on the back of their neck stand up.

On the horizon was a sail.

Based on an idea in Walker Percy's essay 'The Message in the Bottle', New York, 1975

2

Is Christianity for those who can't get a life?

What they say

- Christianity is for losers. It isn't for people who know how to make a success of their lives; it's for stragglers and strugglers.
- Without putting too fine a point upon it, religion seems to be committed to keeping people immature and dependent. We can cope with the major issues of life now without recourse to God.
- Christianity has been overtaken and left behind, at least in the West. We've developed beyond the fears and uncertainties that gave it such a hold in previous centuries.
- Christians are becoming more and more a culturally isolated group of older people. Most ordinary people wouldn't even think of going to church on a Sunday.

* *

Star quote

Organised religion has sunk pretty low these days; the feeling is that it's just third-raters who get involved, oily little tin-pot careerists or neurotics, people afraid of the modern world. A twentieth century Cardinal Wolsey would be a film producer, or an advertising mogul; Sir Thomas More would be a regular guest on late-night talk shows. These guys were big time; you can't imagine them organising coffee mornings or creeping from door to door irritating housewives, can you?

William Leith, Independent on Sunday

* *

Key issue

To many people in the West, Christianity seems as if it's part of yesterday's world. They see it as intellectually superseded by new knowledge, particularly in fields such as high-energy physics, bio-chemistry and psychology. They see it as morally rigid, holding dogmatic beliefs, and out of touch with fast-moving contemporary debates. And they see it as personally restrictive in an age when self-determination and tolerance have been raised to the level of moral absolutes. Christianity is yesterday's brand and can safely be left to fade away.

What you might say

Our world-view is Western, wealthy and very limited. Our slice of 'life' is really quite narrow when you consider that across the world as a whole only one person in a hundred goes to college or has a computer, and only one in four has ever used a telephone. But on this larger map of the world the Christian Church is growing at the rate of about 70,000 new adherents every day (net growth). The Church is certainly struggling in the West, and with our superior Western attitude we're tempted to think that where we go everyone else will eventually follow. But the average Christian now isn't white, Western and middle-aged, but black, young and female – and doesn't speak English. To these Christians it's truly amazing to see how lightly we in the West are discarding the treasures of faith.

All religions, including Christianity, have to take seriously the charge that they keep people immature. In letters written from a German prison camp in the Second World War the theologian Dietrich Bonhoeffer gave the same warning. In a profound sense, he said, humanity has come of age, and to try to keep people in adolescence is pointless, ignoble and un-Christian. However, we need to remember that Christians use the word 'dependent' as a metaphor to describe the appropriate way of relating to the One who holds all things in being. It's like being 'dependent' on the ground we walk on or the air we breathe. In other words it's

11

simply the most common-sense way to live. It doesn't mean sacrificing our intellectual maturity; it's about acknowledging reality.

Moreover, 'obedience to God's commands' (quoted as another sign of immaturity) doesn't mean submitting to an arbitrary set of time-expired commands from a tired old despot; it means acknowledging that certain things make a moral claim on us – they matter, and have a right to matter. It's not good enough to construct our own set of likes and dislikes as if we're choosing what we want from a moral buffet. That could lead to someone saying that while you like being generous and helping people, he likes paedophilia and torture. No, moral demands are recognized as having a claim on us; they're both right and true, and seen in that light, our response is appropriately one of 'obedience'. God isn't into naked power; his only desire is that we should have the best we can in life, and that comes from growing in the way of love, which gets broken down into 'commands' or 'best actions' to guide us.

If the charge is that Christians are people who can't get a life, there's a big question about what 'life' really is. Christians say it's all-inclusive. There's a danger that in constructing our own lives as we like, we leave out of them anything that doesn't give immediate pleasure or that might ask awkward questions of us. A culture dedicated to the pursuit of plea-sure as an end in itself will seriously limit the range of what life holds. More seriously, if life is a consumer free-for-all, we'll exclude millions of people in less developed countries from having a stake. If someone has a stroke or is wasting away with cancer, does that life cease to have meaning or value? Are the millions of destitute people around the world air-brushed out of what 'life' means? In the end we all fall to the dimin-ishments of old age and, according to the colour supplements and the advertisers, we then cease to have value. But a Christian evaluation of life offers infinite value to every human being at every stage of life. Our value is not reduced to a simplistic calculus of pleasure and pain (pleasure = 10; pain = 0). Communities of faith hold a deep wisdom about these things. They know that a framework of beliefs and values, held in community, gives shape and purpose to our lives – whatever the circumstances and conditions. 'Life' includes everything, not just the nice bits.

Another aspect of the 'all-inclusive' nature of life as understood by people of faith relates to the eccentric nature of churches and their congregations. One of the most intriguing facts about Christianity is that it seems to appeal to both the sharpest minds and the simplest souls. You can engage with the Christian faith at any level and find it speaking truthfully and making sense, and that creates a remarkable bond between people of very different backgrounds. I once went to a church which had in the same congregation professors, senior managers, solicitors and teachers, as well as factory workers, students, the unemployed, those with mental disabilities and many others – all delightfully God's family in that place. There was Frank – a small, rather sad man washed up by the tide of unemployment, Mr Nixon – a doughty ex-canal worker who'd lived rough for years and now proudly occupied an outhouse, Barbara – an overlarge, cheerful, down-to-earth Brummie with more illnesses than the average hospital. Together we were the people of God, dedicated to worshipping, learning and serving together. This picture of the multi-dimensional, rainbow people of God is a much more compelling vision of how to 'get a life' than any offered by our contemporary 'lifestyle' gurus.

If we're concerned that Christianity is for people who can't get a life, we need to put into the balance the countless number of artists, musicians, scientists, social reformers, politicians, writers and others who have hugely enriched our culture precisely on the basis of the faith that has inspired and excited them. Here is a record of 'life-giving' which is often forgotten. Bach wrote on every score he composed 'Soli Deo gloria' – to God alone be the glory. Rembrandt's paintings became increasingly profound as his faith deepened. Above the entrance to the Cavendish Science laboratory in Cambridge are inscribed the words 'The works of the Lord are great, sought out by all who have pleasure therein.' The overthrow of both apartheid and communism was largely inspired by men and women of faith. Throughout history Christian faith has inspired works of genius, creativity and social transformation. And even better, faith has inspired a million acts of love, compassion and justice every day, all over the world.

The heart of the matter

Worldwide, the Christian faith attracts all sorts and conditions of people – and in very large numbers. We need to resist being seduced by the narrow view of reality we gain from twenty-first century Britain. Far from Christians needing to 'get a life', it's in order to 'get a life' that millions of people are drawn to Jesus Christ and his extraordinary family.

Quotes for the conversation

My unbelief does not mean that I could do without churches. Perhaps it's in its declining years but Christianity has been responsible for me. The poetry I value, the art that is important to me, have all existed in a Christian framework and can't be understood without reference to Christian beliefs . . . The politics that I have adopted come from the Sermon on the Mount by way of Victorian Christian Socialism. For this reason, if for no other, Christianity has to be treasured and learnt.

John Mortimer, playwright

I believe in Christianity as I believe the sun has risen, not only because I see it, but because by it, I see everything else.

C. S. Lewis, scholar and writer

There are plenty of stories about thirsty people searching for water. One of the great things about Christianity is that it's about the water searching for the thirsty.

After Simon Parke, writer

Christianity is not a theory or a speculation but a life; not a philosophy of life but a life and a living process . . . Try it!

Samuel Taylor Coleridge, poet

God is always the life-bringer. Therefore the heart of the Christian faith is not threat but invitation.

Alan Bartlett, theological educator

The choice for every human being is between death or death, the death of a letting-go that hurts like hell but leads to resurrection, or the death of slow extinction as all the energies are spent on getting and keeping, instead of living and giving.

John V. Taylor, bishop and theologian

Story

Writer A. A. Gill being interviewed:

The interviewer did the Columbo thing of being gauche and cunningly hopeless. 'Sorry, I know I'm being stupid, but can you tell me again: how bad a junkie were you?' I don't make a habit of talking about my days of wine and poppies. It's not that I mind people knowing, it's just that if there's one thing more boring than listening to a drunk, it's listening to a reformed drunk. In passing, really without thinking, I mentioned that I was a Christian.

Well, that did it. The interviewer almost inhaled her asparagus, her eyebrows shot off the top of her head. Nostrils bulging, she waved her arms as if for a passing lifeboat. 'A Christian,' she gasped, Lady Bracknell style. 'A Christian, as in believing in God, the God, that God?' Oh dear. Yes, that God. 'You're not, you can't possibly be.' Now remember, she'd just found out that I'd been a drug dealer, spent adult years smoking cigarettes out of the gutter, sleeping in dog baskets and drinking Benylin and vodka through a straw for breakfast, all of which had elicited no more than an encouraging ho-hum.

This, after all, was only the tired, repetitive litany of contemporary celebrity revelation, but being a Christian and working in the media in the twenty-first century – being someone who's been to the Groucho, eats at the Ivy, is known to public relations VIP lists – how could you possibly be anything as embarrassingly naff and hick and unbelievable as a believer? Well, there it is. I'm outed, proud to be godly . . . Oh, how I wish I could be on the smart, chic, cool team!

15

What does annoy me is when agnostics tell me that my faith is based on superstition and fear, a fear of death, fear of responsibility, that it's an easy option. You think this is easy? You think that the weight of all that paternal expectation is easy? And you imagine that knowing there might be a reckoning in the end makes morality easy? Get a life! Get a faith! It's knowing that ultimately you're your own policeman, judge and jury that's easy, and I wish I could do it.

If I'm honest, I don't miss going into a church and seeing only a pretty building, singing hymns only as raucous songs, standing in front of a Giotto and Titian and seeing merely paintings, or watching my children sleep and having nothing to pray to or to thank. And if you think that's just more of the same nebulous, sentimental, intellectually bereft old hogwash, then tough, I'm not arguing on your terms any more.

3

Why should I be interested?

What they say

- I've got most of the things I want in life. I could always do with more, of course, but basically, life's fine as it is.
- I haven't noticed there's anything missing from my life, really. I don't see what your Christian faith has got to offer me.
- What is it about Christianity that makes it important? I just can't see where it might make contact with my life and what I'm interested in.

***

Star quote

I don't even know I'm going to say the words until they come out of my mouth, and when they do I feel slightly faint. Perhaps I was feeling faint already – it is Sunday morning, and I have not yet eaten. Perhaps if I'd had a bowl of cereal I would never have said anything. 'I'm going to church. Does anyone want to come?'

David and the children look at me with some interest, for some time. It's as if, having said something eccentric, I might follow this up by doing something eccentric, like stripping naked or running amok with a kitchen knife. I am suddenly glad that it is not my job to convince people that going to church is a perfectly healthy leisure activity.

From How to be Good *by Nick Hornby*

***

Key issue

There was a time when Christianity was part of the wallpaper of Western society. It was part of family life and its transitions; it was part of the round of the seasons and our response to nature; it was part of the art and poetry of the culture. Contemporary society doesn't have the same air to breathe; the Christian assumptions have gone. The question people ask in a consumer-driven culture is 'What's in it for me?'

What you might say

Faith is important because it asks the question about meaning, and try as we may to do without it, that question keeps returning. Is life – and my life in particular – a meaningless accident, or is there some purpose to it that makes it worthwhile? Most people feel instinctively that their lives must have a meaning, even if it doesn't keep them awake at night. The trouble is that we often only grasp the meaning of something when we get to the end. For example, when I first met my future wife I had no idea of the meaning and significance of that meeting at the time. Otherwise I might have been more chivalrous! But human beings are natural makers of meaning; we need to know what our lives add up to. Christianity suggests an answer: we have meaning – huge, astonishing, and extraordinary meaning – as children of God, made in the image of God, and made for his love – eternally.

Faith is also important because it asks the question about truth. What is the truth about a human life? Is it made for God or not? Christian faith maintains that we are indeed made for God and will be incomplete in a vital dimension (not an optional one) without him. St Augustine said in a prayer: 'You have made us for yourself and our hearts are restless until they find their rest in you.' That's a truth-claim, not a lifestyle choice. It's not simply a religious 'add-on' to a life that's already going reasonably well. That claim can't be proved, of course, but it does seem that the human heart is programmed for a spiritual search. And just as the object of other human yearnings actually exists (food for the instinct of hunger, sex for the instinct of desire), so we may be inclined to believe there is an object for our spiritual longings. This steady tug in the heart needs something substantial to satisfy it. As one writer put it, 'You can't rely on candyfloss to deal with malnutrition.' Only the Lord of sea and sky will do for our spiritual longings. Perhaps the truth is that we have a kind of spiritual DNA that won't be satisfied until we're embraced by God.

Faith is also important because it asks the question about living – 'how to be good.' How, then, should we live? It's the question that faces us all the time, with every decision we take. It isn't only a political question; it's a personal one, and it requires some framework of priorities and values so that we don't have to begin again with every single decision we face. The belief and value frameworks of the various faith communities have for century after century offered coherent accounts of what it is to live well with our neighbour. These accounts have been about loving and sharing, about justice and mercy, about community and responsibility, about inclusion and peacemaking. And historically, societies haven't been able to think of anything better than these life-enhancing ways of living. If we want to know why we should be interested in faith, here is a clear answer – it helps us to live our lives better. Obviously, different religions have at different times led their followers into acts of appalling darkness (see chapter 4), but that only demonstrates how important and powerful the spiritual DNA is. The spiritual impulse at the heart of faith is characterized by the great Christian trio of love, joy and peace, or loving God and loving our neighbour. How then shall we live? Like that!

Faith is also important because it asks the question about community – 'how to be good' together. Every society has been tested at this crucial point of how to live together in peace and harmony. Ours is becoming a truly fragmented society where people live lonelier lives, eat alone (in front of a screen), have short-term relationships, work in short-term contracts and experience utilitarian friendships. The task of humanity, however, is always to live together generously and in peace. The great religious traditions have a great deal of wisdom in this area. In many parts of the country only the churches offer a comprehensive community, a place where everyone is welcome and where community life can be celebrated. Which is why churches are needed when there's a festival to hold, an anniversary to celebrate or a loss to mourn. Churches are places of hospitality and reconciliation (at least, that's what it says on the tin!) and they draw on thousands of years of learning to live together.

The heart of the matter

The question 'Why should I be interested?' sounds dangerously as if all of life can be reduced to consumer transactions. Life is primarily about developing and sustaining relationships with each other, with the community, with the environment and with God. However, taking the question at face value, there are real benefits in taking Christianity seriously because faith will ask questions about four crucial dimensions of life – meaning, truth, 'how to be good', and how to live together in community. And to each question it proposes an answer which millions of people have experienced as a profound gift.

Quotes for the conversation

I was what you would call at the top of my world. I'd won a Golden Globe for *Evita*, I was pregnant, I had fame, I had fortune, everything that you would perceive a person would want in life. But I'm sure everyone's had that out-of-body experience where you say to yourself – and it might happen at 28 or 38 or 68 – why am I here? Why am I inside this body? What am I doing?

Madonna, singer and actress

All that matters is to be at one with the living God.

D. H. Lawrence, writer

The one thing that is truly worthwhile is becoming God's friend.

Gregory of Nyssa, fourth-century bishop

Hand the remote control over to [the children] if you must. But what will happen when, tired of accruing facts, jargon, logos, trivia, soundbites and cool material trophies, weary of the quick fix and the noise and rush of people skimming between experiences in case they're missing something more exciting, [what if] they dare to stop and reflect and ask us: 'If life is only about getting from now until death as lucratively and divertingly as possible – what is the point? Why didn't you prepare us for the questions? How do I access immortality.com?'

Imogen Stubbs, actress

We had the experience, but missed the meaning.

T. S. Eliot, poet and playwright

If you want to know who I am, don't ask me where I live and what I do, but rather ask me what I am living for, and ask me in very small particulars why I am doing so little about it.

Thomas Merton, monk and writer

The greatest challenge, as Judaism has seen it, is not to ascend from earth to heaven through the journey of the soul, but to bring the Divine presence from heaven to earth and share it with others.

Jonathan Sacks, Chief Rabbi

Story

A wandering holy man settled down at dusk under a tree, near a big rock, beside a path, at the foot of a mountain. He was going to spend the night there, with a stone for a pillow. His meditations were disturbed by a businessman who came running up to him in a very agitated state. 'It must be you!' he said. 'I had a dream last night telling me to come to this tree, near the big rock, beside the path, at the foot of the mountain. Here a wandering holy man would give me a priceless stone and I'd be rich for ever. I've been searching all day, and I'm sure it must be you!'

'Well,' said the holy man, rummaging in his bag, 'perhaps this jewel is the stone from your dream. I saw it on the path the other day. Do take it.' The businessman's mouth dropped open. The diamond was huge!

He couldn't believe it. He carried it home, just bursting with delight. But the feeling didn't last, and by the end of the evening he was deeply troubled. He tossed and turned all night, and he couldn't get off to sleep. He wanted to plan a wonderful new future, but somehow he couldn't get that wandering holy man out of his mind.

Before dawn he got up and went back to the tree, near the big rock, beside the path, at the foot of the mountain. Disturbing the holy man's morning meditation, he laid the diamond on the ground before him. 'Please,' he said, 'can I have the precious gift that allowed you to give away this stone?'

4

The failures of Christianity

There's not much point in constantly asserting that nothing has gone wrong with Christianity. The history of the Christian faith, as of others, has been a mixed bag of glory and dirt, and there's limited value in trying to persuade a sceptical world that it should get over its prejudices and think straight. Indeed Christians can't engage with integrity with people on a spiritual search without having taken seriously the legitimate hostility to Christianity that many people feel. So let's face the failures of Christianity honestly – and then say a word or two that might soften the blow.

* * *

What they say

Far from being a source of peace and justice, Christianity has been the cause of huge suffering in the world.

What you might say

Yes, it has. We need only cite the Crusades, the Inquisition, Northern Ireland, and former Yugoslavia to realize there has been a very dark seam running through Christian history. Support for racism – official in South Africa and unofficial in the southern States – was a stain that took decades to remove. And how clearly did the churches name the demon in Nazism? Christianity must come out with its hands up.

However, we mustn't make superficial judgements about some of these terrible periods of Christian history. The Crusades, for example, were the result of many complex factors that were political, economic and social as well as religious. Nor must we too easily bring the behaviour and beliefs of the past to the bar of the present. The concept of the chivalrous knight laying down his life for his faith was a noble ideal for many centuries; it's not what motivates a modern peace-keeping army but it was legitimate in its time and place. Moreover, religion often gets the blame unfairly instead of nationalism. In Northern Ireland and former Yugoslavia, religion has mainly served as a badge of tribal identity; it hasn't been the deep cause of the conflicts.

Jonathan Swift wrote, 'We have just enough religion to make us hate, but not enough to make us love one another.' The answer then is not less religion but more; a deeper, purified faith which sees that the heart of Christianity, and other faiths, rests in love, mercy and friendship with God. Religions must make sure they have built-in mechanisms for self-criticism, especially critiques that can pull down the idols we constantly create as we make absolutes out of the wrong things – *our* faith community, *our* way of interpreting the holy book, *our* way of living the faith. Because, more positively, there's a growing recognition of the significance of religion in human affairs and that *true* religion is a vital factor in ensuring peace in the world, for at the heart of all true religion is a profound commitment to peace and human flourishing.

* * *

What they say

There's a growing fundamentalism around in many world faiths, and frankly, it's terrifying.

What you might say

I feel the same. Fundamentalism is a problem in Islam, as terrorists claim divine sanction for suicide bombings, but it's also a problem in Christianity where, for example, many Christians line up behind ultra-orthodox Jews in claiming all the lands of the Bible as given by God to them alone. When people believe their faith gives them sanction to kill large numbers of innocent people or to impose their will on a people by force, then religion is acting in its basest way. It's tempting to say it's unforgivable.

The basic issue here is humanity's ability to distort its highest ideals and achievements. If you take any essential human good, such as love or the desire to protect others, and twist it far enough, you come to a point where the good collapses into distortion and becomes a complete corruption of itself. Love twisted far enough can degenerate into lust and abuse. The desire to protect others can become vengeance and 'getting your retaliation in first'. It can happen to all essentially good things. Courage can become irresponsibility, eating can become gluttony, social drinking can become violent mayhem, admiration can become obsession, friendship can become possessiveness. And, in particular, religious faith can become fanatical prejudice. The quality isn't wrong in itself; indeed it's deeply good. The problem comes in the twisting.

Jonathan Sacks, the Chief Rabbi, wrote that 'the only force equal to a fundamentalism of hate is a fundamentalism of love'. All people of true faith would agree with that. And that, of course, is the faith that, in many forms, has offered the world acts of love, compassion, mercy and justice by the million through the centuries. It isn't the faith itself which is at fault; it's the corruption of it. Just because a garden grows weeds, that's no reason to cover it over with concrete.

* * *

What they say

The Church is incredibly socially conservative. Its attitude to women and to gay people puts it right at the back of the queue.

What you might say

The rest of society looks on at the contortions of the Church over its attitude to women as priests or bishops, or actively gay people being ordained, and wonders how out-of-touch does an institution have to be before it wobbles off the planet. It's not a pretty sight, and when you compare it with moral imperatives about world poverty or the environment, it appears little short of irresponsible. Many people have come to think that the moral values of their own lives are far more convincing than this outdated religious system that has simply failed to keep in touch with hard ethical thinking. They may even regard the Church's teaching on a number of issues as positively immoral.

Radical Christians will rightly want the Church to act as the head-lights of society, charting a prophetic course into the future. Others see the Church as acting more like the brake lights, warning society when it's about to get into trouble. The truth is that both are necessary. Some of the greatest moral advances in society have come from the enlightened thinking of Christians who have looked at the far-reaching teachings of the New Testament and applied them to issues such as slavery, apartheid, the treatment of children in factories, the need for hospitals, schools and care for the terminally ill, and so on. 'But why were some reforms so long in the coming?' some will ask, and the answer is that what's ethically clear to us has often had to ripen over time. Or, to change the metaphor, the New Testament teaching has sometimes been like a slow-burning fuse which has only latterly reached the point of explosion. At other times the Church has acted like brake lights, counselling caution when, for example, the dignity of individual lives created in the image of God has been under urgent threat, as in the continuing debates on abortion, euthanasia or human cloning.

This still doesn't account for the particular issues of the ordination of women and gay people. If these debates are couched only in terms of human rights then the Church's convolutions are indeed ludicrous. But the Church's contention is that it isn't bound to be swept along in the secular flood but has to evaluate such issues theologically, with a range of different data to consider, drawn from the memory banks of our great moral traditions. After all, the Church doesn't think in terms of political and cultural pragmatism; it thinks in terms of fundamental truths about humankind, and it measures its thinking not in parliamentary sessions but in centuries of wise deliberation. That's not to say that society isn't right in these cases and the Church is being hopelessly cautious; it's simply to say that the arguments have a somewhat different framework, and in the long run, that may be what society needs.

* * *

What they say

Part of the underlying structure of Christianity is deeply negative. It induces guilt; it threatens judgement; it's fundamentally anti-life.

What you might say

Indeed that's how Christianity has come across to vast numbers of people. No matter that Jesus said 'I have come that they may have life, and have it abundantly'; no matter that the goal of humanity is to 'enjoy God for ever' and that Irenaeus said 'The glory of God is a human person fully alive.' People have nevertheless experienced the Christian faith as diminishing their lives and constricting them. They've been made to feel a 'miserable sinner'.

Of course what has been happening in the last hundred years has been the almost universal loss of a sense of sin. More relaxed attitudes to personal behaviour have grown rapidly and there is much less confidence in the objectivity of moral judgements. Moreover, the reality of God has sunk below the skyline for most people; we live with a kind of functional atheism. At the same time, this has been a period in which some of the most terrible things in human history have been happening, things which one would have expected to shake even the most self-confident society. The Nazi Holocaust, Stalin's killing of 28 million people, nearly a million hacked to death by their neighbours in Rwanda, the Armenian genocide, Idi Amin, Saddam Hussein, Bosnia, Kosovo, 9/11, Bali, Beslan – the tragic litany scorches the memory. Is there not room for some humility before the terrible face of human cruelty? All is not well with the human condition.

A balance is needed here. Society is right to complain if the Church forgets that Creation came first, a joyful, life-giving creation made out of God's sheer delight. 'God saw everything that he had made and indeed it was very good' (Genesis 1.31). People are right to mutter darkly if the Church seems to condemn everything new that they experience as life-giving. If any one thing most attracted me to Christian faith it was the enormous capacity for life that I saw and sensed in Jesus of Nazareth, and found confirmed in the resurrection. On the other hand, our human capacity for evil is unlimited and needs to be confronted with the call for recognition and repentance. And the Church doesn't serve God or humanity if it fails to hold up a challenging mirror to society when it chants those familiar mantras of 'Do your own thing', 'Whatever works for you', 'If it feels good, do it'. That's no way to run anything, from a family to a company or a nation. Certainly there are huge dilemmas in contemporary society, but the fact of their existence no more disproves the existence of objective moral standards than the fact that some things are grey disproves the existence of black and white.

Affirmation and challenge. That's what the Church should aim for, not blanket negativity. It may not always be popular; it won't always get it right; but it will be offering society the invaluable company of a critical and hopeful friend.

* * *

What they say

Some Christianity is sheer intellectual nonsense.

What you might say

I have a good deal of sympathy with this critique. Some versions of the Christian faith make me cringe and they lead intelligent people to conclude that the only serious option for an honest, thinking, scientifically informed person is atheism, or maybe if they're generous, agnosticism. Creationism is an intellectual disaster area, making Christian faith seem obscurantist and absurd. Going up a hilltop and waiting for the end of the world because of an eccentric reading of Revelation and the signs of the times is simply embarrassing. Praying for a broken leg not to be broken or for the sun to shine on my birthday (when the farmers need rain), praying for my lost car keys or a parking space – all these trivialize the grace of God and the dignity of prayer.

It's more difficult to see what can be done about these excesses. On the positive side, God isn't proud, and he loves each one of his extraordinary children with an equal, undivided love. And who among us can cast the first stone? There will be things about some of my beliefs that will strike others as ridiculous; they're just too polite to tell me. But it also points to the need for each church to have programmes of Christian education that genuinely stretch people and don't just reinforce superficiality. All I can say to my honest sceptical friend is: don't shoot the piano player; listen to the music.

5

Life in a spiritual supermarket

What they say

- More and more of us describe ourselves as 'spiritual' and fewer and fewer as 'religious'. Twice as many people believe in a spiritual force within them as believe in a personal God beyond them. And two-thirds of 18–24-year-olds have more belief in their horoscopes than in the Bible.
- 'In spirituality, gurus are our cocktail shakers – mixing up a bit of Buddhism, a touch of Kabbalah, some feng shui, a dash of Wicca and a pinch of shamanism. So where does that leave our traditional religious leaders with their old-fashioned, single-brand approach to theism? Increasingly obsolete.' The Times, *October 2004*
- 'To me the concept of institutionalised religion is dated. Spirituality is about being connected, learning to be a good person, not obeying arcane rules or believing in one truth. Who cares whether it's Christ or Krishna? They're just different archetypes of the same mythology.' *33-year-old fashion stylist,* The Times, *May 2003*
- 'About 50 per cent of the people I see were brought up quite religiously, so the seed of spirituality was there but the Church wasn't fulfilling their spiritual need. People are less inclined just to accept what they are told; they need to know it for themselves.' *44-year-old t'ai chi practitioner, raised in Church of England*
- Apple schedules a 30 minute meditation break for its employees, and the management consultancy McKinsey is sending its executives on spiritual intelligence courses. The World Bank holds regular meetings for its Spiritual Unfoldment Society to discuss meditation, reincarnation and the like. Orange has had its UK headquarters feng-shuied, and Kwik-Fit provides its employees with a chill-out club, t'ai chi and yoga. Sunday Times, *April 2005*

```
* * * * * * * * * * * * * * * * * * * * * * * * * * * * * * * * *
*                                                               *
*  Star quote                                                   *
*                                                               *
*  'The things I've believed all my life – about sin and redemption *
*  and the mortification of the body – you'd say none of those things *
*  mean anything, wouldn't you?'                                *
*     'I'd say that you are entitled to your beliefs. As long as they *
*  make you happy.'                                             *
*     'And what – if it isn't an impertinent question – what do you *
*  believe?'                                                    *
*     Magic carpet rides, rune magic, Ali Baba and visions of  *
*  the Holy Mother, astral travel and the future in the dregs of a *
*  glass of red wine. Buddha. Frodo's journey into Mordor. The *
*  transubstantiation of the sacrament. Dorothy and Toto. The  *
*  Easter Bunny. Space aliens. The Thing in the closet. The Resur- *
*  rection and the Life at the turn of a card . . . I've believed them *
*  all at one time or another. Or pretended to. Or pretended   *
*  not to.                                                      *
*     And now? What do I believe right now?                     *
*     'I believe that being happy is the only important thing,' I told *
*  him at last.                                                 *
*     Happiness. Simple as a glass of chocolate or tortuous as the *
*  heart. Bitter. Sweet. Alive.                                 *
*                                   Joanne Harris, Chocolat     *
*                                                               *
* * * * * * * * * * * * * * * * * * * * * * * * * * * * * * * * *
```

Key issue

This is undeniably an age when spirituality is back on the radar screen. There's no need to be apologetic about raising issues of spirituality in almost any quarter of society. However, the idea of spirituality has become divorced in people's minds from what the Church has to offer. Spirituality and religion are seen not just as belonging in separate compartments but almost as opposites, spirituality representing freedom, discovery and life; religion representing rules, fear and repression.

What you might say

To separate out religion and spirituality is to cut ourselves off from a huge, rich spiritual tradition. In the Christian faith we've had two thousand years of profound meditation on the meaning and nature of God. We've had the greatest minds and the loveliest souls plumbing the depths of the human spirit. We've had prayer, poetry, music, art and spiritual wisdom of every kind pouring out of the Christian tradition. We've had saints experiencing the heights of spiritual ecstasy and the depths of the dark night of the soul. We've explored scripture and silence, learning and liturgy; we've written hymns by the hundred thousand; we've built some of the finest buildings on earth; we've followed the divine scent into monasteries and mountains, into deserts and cities. It's impossible to separate spirituality and religion.

There is, however, a distinction between the two. It's as if spirituality is the poetry of the soul and religion is the prose. Spirituality is the direct encounter with God; religion is the set of activities we establish to sustain that encounter and support the group of people who have had that encounter. It's like the relationship between love and marriage. One can exist without the other, but love is the emotion (the 'direct encounter') while marriage is the institution that sustains that emotional encounter. In an age that values emotions above institutions, we seek love rather than marriage, spirituality rather than religion. But institutions are important because they give permanence to what might otherwise be a fleeting experience. They give stability and continuity. They express publicly what would otherwise just be private. We need both poetry and prose, passion and routine, in our marriage and in our experience of the divine.

The danger of a 'pick 'n' mix' approach to the spiritual journey is that it ends up in confusion. Our major religions are coherent. They offer powerful narratives, beliefs, rituals and symbols that are internally consistent, and to drift along the supermarket shelves, picking up a bit of feng shui here and a smattering of Buddhism there, treats spirituality and religion as mere consumer items. Constructing our own selves by seeking wisdom wherever we can find it and bolting bits together in random fashion sounds like a common-sense approach, but it's in danger of leaving us short-changed and bewildered. The hungry soul won't be fed; it will only be entertained.

The essence of spirituality and religion is that we enter a bigger world, an ancient wisdom, an arena of rugged truth and wild beauty. It's not a fashion accessory. Its core value is that we can't control it – it takes us over, and we are the object, not the subject. Many contemporary 'spiritualities' seem to be more like 'do-it-yourself', flat-packed, 'easy assembly' programmes for more-or-less instant happiness. They may last for a while but the novelty wears off and a new fad emerges. By contrast, the major faiths offer something much bigger than our familiar world of disposable goods and re-cycled experiences. These faith traditions de-stabilize us, excite and subvert us, take us to depths we've never previously examined; they introduce us to landscapes beyond our imagining. And above all they free us from the tyranny of the present, and place us in the much longer narrative of past, present and future.

When spirituality and religion are fused together you have a resource that society both needs and tacitly recognizes. People turn to the Church to handle their major traumas and transitions, whether they be the terrorist attack of 9/11, the death of a royal or the murder of young innocents, or the more domestic but equally life-changing events of having a child, getting married or facing death. Twelve million people visit our cathedrals each year, clearly experiencing something that matters to them. In the national census of 2001, in the privacy of their own homes, 71 per cent of British people still wanted to tick the box marked 'Christian'. They could have said 'No religion' or even put 'Jedi Knight' but they still wanted to identify with this way of life. Instinctively very large numbers of people know that the Christian faith and its spiritual tradition is a huge resource of meaning and strength.

Christianity actually makes a rather powerful critique of contemporary 'no-cost', 'easy access' spiritualities. The lonely, battered figure on a cross puts a big question-mark against all our self-help, soft-centred spiritualities. The German theologian Dietrich Bonhoeffer, who died at the hands of the Nazis for his part in the attempt on Hitler's life, wrote of the danger of 'cheap grace'. By this he meant that grace which costs nothing ends up counting for nothing and achieving nothing. On the other hand, the grace of God cost the life of Jesus. There's a parallel in the huge number of people who join gyms, and the very great proportion of them who give up after three months. When the implications become clear (hard work, time and sweat) most people move on. The real benefits only become apparent with the application of character and determination. So too in the realm of the spirit – there's no cheap grace.

The heart of the matter

The forgotten riches of the Christian spiritual tradition are able to offer a profound and coherent framework for puzzled humanity. Most people now realize that the secular, materialist dream is a fantasy. But the alternative isn't to construct a jumble-sale spirituality of bits and pieces. Rather it's to enter and inhabit a faith tradition that offers depth, continuity and imagination. Ultimately pick 'n' mix spirituality won't satisfy because it places the individual at the centre, and any faith where the highest being is oneself is clearly limited. If we try to 'do God' on our own terms the spiritual life is about what 'God' can do for us and how we can mould him to our own needs. Christianity is saying the opposite.

Quotes for the conversation

The inner life is called the soul, and the art of knowing it, healing it, and harmonising its forces, is called spirituality.

Gerard Hughes, spiritual writer

The Christian ideal has not been tried and found wanting; it has been found difficult and not tried.

G. K. Chesterton, author

The one great solid rock of the sacred has been first shattered (by the Reformation) and then fragmented and pulverised into small pieces of rubble – 'small incoherent beliefs in crystals, pyramids, feng shui, shiatsu, copper wire, spirit-writing, drugs – peddled to people who know they need something invisible in their lives but don't know what.'

Libby Purves, journalist and novelist

Churches, not just New Age seminars, could respond directly to the obvious spiritual hunger across the land and be less afraid of its excesses. Congregations can become the much needed places of spiritual formation that our society desperately lacks, stressing character over success, spirituality over consumption, fidelity over gratification, honesty over expediency, leadership over celebrity, and integrity over everything else.

Jim Wallis, Christian social activist

Story

A former political lobbyist, Derek Draper, became clinically depressed when his habits of clubbing, cocaine abuse and Ecstasy were compounded by a lobbying scandal that forced him to resign. His therapist advised him to include spirituality in his balance of life, and he took up yoga, Reiki and some New Age remedies. He decided to look at Buddhism and went to meetings and read a couple of books by the Dalai Lama. But then something strange happened when he went into a church. His words:

Next to Westminster Abbey there's a beautiful little church. In five years of working in Parliament I don't think I had ever really noticed it. I gazed at the altar for a moment and then lowered my head and closed my eyes. Instantly I became conscious of how quiet the church was. I breathed deeply and, to my amazement, I started to have the same feelings I had when doing yoga or Reiki – a sense of my non-physical self unfolding, stretching out, being at peace. It occurred to me that maybe I was feeling what people call the presence of God. I don't suppose I knew what 'prayer' really was, so I found myself reciting the Lord's Prayer, remembered from two decades earlier. Then I found prayer coming so naturally that I felt as you do when you wake from a nightmare and momentarily cannot breathe, then suddenly take a great gulp of air. Released. Heard.

A few days later he found himself going to church in Primrose Hill, the first time he'd been to church since he was thirteen, twenty years before. It was perfect.

The splendour of the robes, the incense and the beautiful choir mix with an informality that was summed up on All Saints Day when two young altar boys mounted the steps with day-glo trainers showing under their cassocks. That first Sunday the vicar, a former Benedictine monk, managed to combine a sermon addressing fear with a genuinely funny joke about Charlie Dimmock. I was hooked.

Derek Draper, The Times, *February 2001*

6

Why Jesus and not Buddha?

What they say

- What's so special about Christianity? We're aware now of the wisdom and richness of so many different world faiths, all with millions of faithful followers, so how can we prioritize any one of them?
- Aren't all religions, at root, saying the same kind of things – about love and mercy and forgiveness and peace? Aren't they all heading in the same direction?
- Christians have a long history of cultural and religious arrogance. All attempts to put Christianity in a privileged position are simply new forms of this instinctive Western imperialism.
- Isn't it better to take the best features from different faiths and apply them to your own life rather than opt into just one world faith?
- If no-one comes to the Father except through Jesus (John 14.6) where does that leave all those billions of good, faithful followers of other faiths through the centuries? Were they all wrong?

Key issue

Christians want to hold to the distinctiveness of Jesus as God's full and final revelation of himself but obviously they don't want to believe that all those of other faiths are outside God's truth and mercy. But if the uniqueness of Christ is conceded the whole Christian edifice may begin to crumble.

What you might say

Let's do some ground-clearing first. It can't possibly be the case that all religions are more or less the same, saying the same things and heading for the same place. That's an insult to the integrity of each of them and no serious adherent of any great faith believes it. They may all be exploring our relationship with the divine but they do so in incredibly different ways. For instance, in Hinduism the divine is impersonal and plural; in Islam the divine is personal and singular; in Buddhism the divine is neither personal nor active, whereas in Christianity it's both. To say all religions are really the same is like saying physics, history and sociology are really the same – they're all concerned with knowledge – and it doesn't matter which you study because they all end up saying the same thing. That wouldn't impress the examiners!

Christians have certainly been arrogant about their faith in the past, and there are still some extraordinary statements that come out of some dark theological corners. What's needed is a renewed theological mind in parts of the Church, and some graceful repentance. On the other hand we mustn't judge our predecessors by the standards of our own theology and cultural norms. Previous ages had their own interpretations of the Christian tradition and need to be judged by their own lights.

Christian thinking about mission and interfaith dialogue has a complex history. In the last few decades a distinction has been drawn between exclusivist, pluralist and inclusivist positions about other faiths. An *exclusivist* would say that unless you could declare that 'Jesus is Lord' you couldn't have a passport to heaven. This view hardly accords with the God and Father of our Lord Jesus Christ who would be unlikely to have left the vast majority of human beings without any knowledge of him. A *pluralist* would say that although all faiths are different in form and content, they're all on a similar footing in relation to ultimate truth, none 'better' than another. This sidesteps all issues of truth and the undoubted incompatibilities of different faiths referred to above. An *inclusivist* would say that echoes of Jesus can be found in other faiths, so followers of other paths might in fact be faithful to Jesus without knowing it – anonymous Christians. The danger here is that we define other religions in exclusively Christian terms, only seeing them in the light of Christianity, and this could be said to be an unfair colonization of them.

Probably a better starting point is to take the Jewish and Greek idea of the *'logos'* or 'Word' of God – the creative, ordering principle in the cosmos – and to work from there. That creative Word is to be found permeating the whole of creation (he 'enlightens everyone', John 1.9), and outcrops of the *logos* will be seen in every culture and faith. Christians believe that the *logos* is seen spectacularly and fully in Jesus Christ, but that doesn't stop them recognizing signs of that Presence in many other places. The beauty, compassion, grace and truth of God, which Christians delight to see fully focused in Jesus, may be seen and enjoyed throughout God's creation, and in particular in its various cultures and faiths. The important point is to maintain a universal understanding of God and his mission of love; we cannot accept less.

Does that mean people of all faiths and none sitting down in the Kingdom of God – Hindus, Muslims, Buddhists, atheists too? It does – but of course not automatically. The *logos* is universal. John says that 'in the Word was life, and the life was the light of *all* people' (John 1.4). Truth, therefore, is indivisible and anyone can encounter it. However – and this is the rub – people's response to the *logos* and its outworkings, in a life of love, mercy, peace, justice and the like, cannot be guaranteed. We are disobedient even to our own faith traditions, and may turn our backs on the way of life, the way of salvation. Christians have found their best hold on the truth to be in the life, death and resurrection of Jesus Christ and will continue to offer that understanding to the world. They will say that 'God proves his love for us in that while we were still sinners, Christ died for us' (Romans 5.8). As for others – that's up to them and God.

How then should Christians relate to those of other faiths? The word always used now is *'dialogue'*. Interfaith dialogue always requires respect. No-one should be looking for opportunities to pounce or they'll never be listening and open to new understanding. We need to encounter each other not with bullet-proof prejudice and cheap shots but with the humility of children of God seeking wisdom from one another. The aim of dialogue isn't superficial consensus; it's honest conversation, seeking new contours of truth from each other, sharing convictions and stories, lowering the boundary walls of suspicion. It doesn't mean holding our own faith with any less conviction but it does mean we should be prepared for personal change and enrichment.

When engaged with people of other faith communities Christians can be assured that Jesus is the Truth. This means that if we pursue the truth in any dialogue it won't be long before we bump into Jesus Christ.

The urgency of dialogue is now becoming ever more evident. Amid the clash of cultures and the reality of a form of global terrorism that claims religious sanction, people of faith have a huge responsibility to engage in dialogues that build understanding and feed peace. These dialogues may be of many kinds:

1 *Dialogues of belief*: on questions of doctrinal interest.
2 *Dialogues of life*: where different faith communities live and grow together.
3 *Dialogues of the spirit*: where people share their spiritual resources and practices.
4 *Dialogues of action*: where communities engage together in concrete actions for justice, peace, the well-being of the living environment and so on.
5 *Institutional dialogue*: where religious traditions meet in interfaith organizations for sustained dialogue and joint action.

The heart of the matter

At a conference on world religions the question being discussed was what was unique to the Christian story. Was it God becoming man? Not completely; other religions had a form of incarnation of the divine. Was it resurrection? No, other faiths had stories of a return from death. Healing, perhaps? No, other religions had plenty of that. And so the debate went on, until C. S. Lewis said simply: 'The answer is grace. That's the difference.'

Grace is the absolutely unconditional, inexhaustible and reckless love of God for us and for all people. It's hard to grasp just

---

how radical that is, so religious people often seem to be agreeing that God loves us but that his acceptance of us still ultimately depends on our own performance, that we have to earn the right to be children of God. But the radicalism of Christian faith is that grace comes first. God has already accepted us as his friends, in spite of everything. He just wants us to accept that acceptance, and let ourselves be loved like that, and so become part of his new creation. Christianity puts grace at the non-negotiable heart of faith. And if that attracts other people to become followers of Jesus – thanks be to God!

Quotes for the conversation

Faith perishes if it is walled in or confined. If it is anywhere, it must be everywhere, like God himself: if God is in your life, he is in all things, for he is God. You must be able to spread the area of your recognition of him and the basis of your conviction about him, as widely as your thought will range.

Austin Farrer, theologian

If we can open our minds and hearts to other religions and see something of Christ in them, then the proper expression of this is thankfulness to God.

Richard Harries, bishop and theologian

A church which is open to the reality of Judaism will be a different and more humble church, but one, I believe, renewed in truth and holiness and more ready, in a suffering world, to share with others the love of God.

Marcus Braybrooke, interfaith writer

[In dialogue with people of other faiths] I shall see past what are to me distasteful rituals, alien symbols and concepts that carry no conviction, to the insights they are trying to express. I shall come to appreciate [the other's] understanding of what a man [*sic*] is, how he is related to his family, to the dead, to the whole of existence, and to the ultimate reality. And, as a final bestowal, I shall be given access to the dark places of that stranger's world – the things that really make him ashamed or anxious or despairing. And then, at last, I shall see the saviour and Lord of *that* world, my Lord Jesus, and yet not as I have known him. I shall understand how perfectly he matches all the needs and all the aspirations and all the insights of that other world – he who is the unique Lord and saviour of all possible worlds. And I shall worship him with a new-found wonder and falteringly start proclaiming him in the new terms which I am just beginning to understand.

John V. Taylor, bishop and missionary

To engage in authentic evangelism [Christians] do not need to deny whatever is true, good and beautiful in human thought, art, technology, structures of society and even spirituality. They need, rather, to affirm that such truth, goodness and beauty are from the eternal *logos*, who is uniquely revealed in Jesus Christ, and find their fulfilment in him.

Michael Nazir-Ali, bishop and theologian

'I greet you in the name of Jesus who to you is a prophet and to me is a Saviour.'

John Sentamu, Archbishop of York,
when he meets people of other faiths

Story

As a young curate in Birmingham I found myself working with a young Buddhist couple – both English – who were also committed to issues of world poverty and development. We were asked round for a meal and saw in the corner of the living room a space clearly set aside for prayer. It turned out that they spent an hour each morning and evening in meditation, gaining strength for their humanitarian task.

When I looked at my own practice of prayer, scrambling a few minutes when I could, I came away deeply humbled. Who had what to teach to whom?

But we didn't talk about what we each thought was the truth that sets us free.

Part Two

WHY BELIEVE?

7

Is there anybody there?

———•◆•———

What they say

- There's no proof. How can you believe in God without any evidence?
- It's a lot of wishful thinking. God didn't make us; we made God. We made him up because we needed a protective Father-figure to believe in.
- All the arguments about God are so flaky. They're all like pink mist; there's nothing to get hold of.
- Belief in God was a primitive idea that we've grown out of. We're on our own and we know it.

* *

Star quote

The idea that there is a personal God who lives somewhere and keeps an eye on us and punishes us and rewards us, is dead. It's not possible to believe that any more. Intellectually the life's gone out of it. It's lying there stiff and cold and empty. God is dead. That's what I'm killing with the death of my God in this [story].

Philip Pullman, author

* *

Key issue

We live in a 'seeing is believing' culture. We only believe in what we can see or prove. People of faith find this frustrating because they think this 'Enlightenment' way of thinking is too restrictive. But at least we know that this is the central issue: is there anybody there? Because if the

45

presumption of God is without foundation then the whole religious edifice collapses into fantasy.

What you might say

Of course there's no way to prove the existence of God. God doesn't 'exist' as one object in a field of objects; God simply 'is'. Previous ages had their arguments which were persuasive at the time but they reflected the philosophies of their day. Believers are now much more careful in what they claim. The arguments we might produce today won't amount to proof (if they did, in a sense, we would be greater than God because we could contain him in our minds), but they're certainly able to demonstrate the reasonableness of belief. The approaches have a cumulative effect. They overlap and interweave like planks of wood making up a raft which eventually you trust enough to keep you afloat as you set off down the river.

Christians claim that God is personal, and you don't *prove* persons – you meet them. Personal knowledge is different from scientific knowledge. It's the form of knowledge applicable to things like courage and hope and love and happiness. You don't measure these qualities and experiences in terms of centimetres and kilos. You don't tell your children you love them 10 centimetres. You could describe love as 'the cognitive-affective state, characterized by intrusive and obsessive fantasizing concerning reciprocity of amorant feeling by the object of the amorance' (a definition used at a conference), but the so-called 'object' of your affections is unlikely to be impressed! Our knowledge of God requires a different language – a personal, poetic, religious language.

The existence of the universe cries out for some kind of explanation. The basic question to ask is why anything exists rather than nothing. And in particular, you need a sufficient explanation for something as massive and mind-boggling as our universe to exist. Believers have called this 'sufficient reason' God, and have seen him as a Creator of genius who was prepared to work with endless patience and enormous risk to let a universe evolve that would reflect his own beauty and creativity.

He creates a universe that creates itself. This isn't a knock-down proof; merely a reasonable deduction from the observable universe. At the end of 2004 the famous philosopher Anthony Flew, a lifelong atheist, went public on changing his mind. For six decades he had argued against the existence of God but now he said he found it impossible to account for the creation of the universe without some idea of God. He still believed there was 'a world of difference between finding that there's some very powerful, intelligent being in the background and finding that what you've discovered is the God of Abraham, Isaac and Israel'. But it's a start!

Developing that line of thinking a stage further, there seem to be a number of scientific reasons which open up the concept of God. What's called the 'anthropic principle' demonstrates that the existence of life on Earth results from extreme fine-tuning in the physical fabric of the universe. For example, if the rate of expansion of the universe had been different by one millionth part, there would be no life on earth. The conditions for the vital manufacture of carbon, on which all life depends, is similarly fine-tuned. There is a huge range of such anthropic balances, and they have led many scientists to see a deep intelligible order in the universe. Professor Paul Davies said, 'It's hard to resist the impression that the present structure of the universe has been rather carefully thought out.' This is a modern version of the old (discredited) argument from design. There's something about the universe that keeps on suggesting a 'Mind' behind it. The anthropic principle does not offer proof of God, but it forms part of an intellectually respectable case for belief in God.

Another striking factor about the universe, in whole or in part, is the sense of awe that it evokes in us so naturally. These are the 'Wow, look at that!' moments when we're stopped in our tracks and seem suddenly to be seeing through a chink in the fabric of creation. The beauty and vastness of the universe have always moved people to religious responses, as has the detail of a flower head or a butterfly's wings. 'When I consider the heavens, the work of your fingers, the moon and stars which you have set into place, what is man that you are mindful of him, the son of man that you care for him?' (Psalm 8) Putting that ancient response in a modern context, astronaut James Irwin saw the earth from space and said, 'seeing this has to change a man, has to make a man appreciate the creation of God and the love of God'. This instinctive response of joy and wonder seems to be drawn out of people of every age and culture. Such a universal experience needs to be taken seriously.

Our moral instinct seems to come at us as a demand from elsewhere, not as something we construct for ourselves. Of course people will have different views on what's right and wrong in particular cultures at particular times. We can all dispute these. But behind these variations is an irrefutable belief shared by practically everybody that certain things *matter*, and moreover that *they have a right to matter*. When a gunman shoots at random in a classroom of little children we don't simply say that we don't like that sort of thing. It's objectively and absolutely wrong. When we think of Gandhi's life in India, Mother Teresa's care for the dying in Calcutta, the life and compassion of Jesus in Palestine, or the heroism of Nelson Mandela in South Africa, and we call them 'good', we're doing more than merely stating a preference; we're talking of actions that are objectively good. So morality seems to be more than personal choice. Certain things confront us, make a claim on us, demand our attention. And where does this objectivity come from? Such an experience is at least consistent with believing in a moral Mind behind the universe. The experience of moral obligation points to a transcendent Source of goodness.

There's a rather slippery thing called 'religious experience' we might want to put into the balance. In 2000 a BBC *Soul of Britain* poll revealed that 76 per cent of those polled reported they had had a religious or spiritual experience (however slippery that concept is). This figure had risen from 48 per cent in a similar poll in 1987. It's true that most of the younger people in that poll would not want to adopt a Christian framework for that experience, but the figure is still remarkable. And yet it's what has been reported from the beginning of time. People have spoken of encountering the numinous, the Other, God, in every culture and in every age. It's a universal phenomenon. Of course it's possible simply to put this down to psychological compensation, but reductionism (the tendency to reduce awkward phenomena to 'nothing but' something else) has always been a poor intellectual tool. If such an instinct has been so widespread and so long-lasting you have to wonder if there isn't some actual reality to which this instinct corresponds. It seems as if human beings are unavoidably religious creatures. According to the strict logic of natural selection, any phenomenon which is so pervasive and persistent must be in our genes. Like it or not, we're born to believe.

There's another argument here which is rather jumping the gun. We haven't yet considered the significance of the giant personality of Jesus. But if we take his testimony as being at all trustworthy, we need to reckon with the fact that his entire life was based on the centrality and utter necessity of God. Everything else Jesus said has stood the test of time and the accumulated experience of millions of people. Why should he be wrong on the most important fact of his life?

The heart of the matter

Humankind could never 'prove' God's existence any more than Hamlet could 'prove' Shakespeare's existence. We operate in a different framework, where we are the subjects in the story, not the Author of it. Nevertheless there are pointers within the created order (the 'story') which encourage the reasonableness of belief and, taken together, make belief for many people irresistible. Finally the question will be along the lines of: 'What picture of reality makes most sense to you – God or no-God?' Or 'Which narrative can you inhabit most confidently?' Faith is then a decision, a choice, but one based on a mass of evidence and experience.

Quotes for the conversation

My religion consists of a humble admiration of the illimitable superior Spirit who reveals himself in the slight details we are able to perceive with our feeble minds. That deeply emotional conviction of the presence of a superior reasoning power which is revealed in the universe, forms my idea of God.

Albert Einstein, scientist

To the post-modern suggestion that something can be 'true-for-me' but not 'true', the following reply can be made. Is fascism as equally true as democratic liberalism? Consider the person who believes, passionately and sincerely, that it is an excellent thing to place millions of Jews in gas chambers. That is certainly 'true-for-him'. But can it be allowed to pass unchallenged? Is it equally true as the belief that one should live in peace and tolerance with one's neighbours?

Alister McGrath, theologian

There's a crisis of confidence gripping atheism. Belief in God was meant to have died out years ago. Everyone knows it has not worked out like that. Instead atheism is trapped in a time warp. What happens when a new interest in spirituality surges through western culture, and when the cultural pressures that once made atheism seem attractive are replaced by others that make it seem intolerant, unimaginative and disconnected from spiritual realities?

Alister McGrath

When we have sacrificed God there is nothing left to worship except stone, stupidity, gravity and fate.

Nietzsche, philosopher

I believe in a little patch of light at the end of a torch beam. The arguments about the Big Bang and the First Cause are valuable and proper intellectual arguments; but the only real apprehension of God is a feeling, a knowledge that he exists. It solves no problems. It doesn't make anyone wise. All you know is there's a light there – a stumbling, fumbling torchlight perception of God.

William Golding, novelist

Everything else can wait, but the search for God can't wait. And love one another.

Final words of George Harrison, former Beatle,
as reported in the press

Story

Carl Jung, the psychotherapist, was counselling a man who'd been in therapy for six months and was getting no better. Finally Dr Jung said, 'Friend, I can't do anything more for you. What you need is God.'

'How do I find God, Dr Jung?' the man asked.

'I don't know,' said Jung, 'but I suspect that if you find a group of people who believe in him passionately and just spend time with them, then you will find God.'

8

The God I don't believe in

What they say

- God seems to be a cross between a megalomaniac and the tooth fairy.
- God's like a celestial football referee: he only interferes to tell you off.
- God seems to be like a disapproving parent, tut-tutting when you make a mistake or commit a sin.
- Maybe God is the ultimate control-freak, trying to impose his will on the world. He's a malevolent despot crushing the joy out of human life.
- God's a smiley Santa, everybody's feel-good friend. Only he's not much use in the bad times.
- God's like a celestial pink mist – 'immortal, invisible, God only wise, in light inaccessible, hid from our eyes'. Too mysterious by half.

* *

Star quote

I am longing for the day when Bishops resign en masse as a protest against the feckless master they have served so long, with so much misplaced trust. Humans, at least, are capable of nobility and altruism, and this makes us morally superior to God, who would appear to be like an Ottoman sultan. He is an absolute despot who is out of control of his empire, surrounded by sycophants, answerable to no-one, drunk with apathy, who demands homage and taxes from his people without offering any services in return.

Louis de Bernières, author, quoted by Richard Harries

* *

Story

I was talking to a group of children about God. 'How old is he?' one asked. 'Very old,' I said. 'A million years?' came back the questioner. 'More than that,' I said. 'He's always been alive.' One little girl thought about this for a while and then she announced sternly, 'He must need a bath soon!'

Key issue

These beliefs about God make him intellectually or morally inconceivable to many thoughtful people. Most Christians would say that the God such people don't believe in, they don't believe in either. And yet many others, even practising Christians, would seem to hold some variant on one or more of these images of God. The important underlying issue is that the image of God people carry with them is massively influential on a whole range of further matters, such as: the way people worship, the way they pray, how they conceive of mission, how they relate to people of other faiths, how they participate in church life, how they care for each other, and so on. Our image of God is a crucial controlling factor in our lives, and is often left unexamined.

What you might say

We're bound to misunderstand what God is like. Any description we come up with is like trying to play a Beethoven symphony on a tin whistle. We don't have the instruments for it. We don't have the language. It's like asking a child in a nursery school what a university is like.

One result of this is that all our language about God is metaphorical. It can't be an exact description; we have to proceed by offering tentative ideas, phrases and images which make a multi-layered and many-angled attempt to say something about God that isn't totally foolish. God, remember, isn't another object in the universe in addition to every other object; he isn't an extra item on an imaginary list of 'things that exist in the universe'. All our descriptions are inadequate metaphors, such as St Augustine's 'God is a circle whose centre is everywhere and whose circumference is nowhere', or the Bible's 'God is a consuming fire.' But we have to use them because we have nothing else.

The problem with talking about God is that either we say too much or too little. We can end up with a verbal riot, heaping image upon image; or we get reduced to stuttering silence, unable to trust ourselves to utter a word about God. The first strategy is called the 'cataphatic way', pushing words and images to their limits. Muslims have 99 names for God – the Sublime, the Subtle, the Compassionate, etc. And the hundredth name is whatever name a desperate person uses when he calls out for God, for God will answer to that name. The other approach is called the 'apophatic way', the mystical way, the way of silence, which at least saves us from saying anything too inadequate and ridiculous.

But if we are to use words, the best image Christians have been able to come up with, and the one that Christian experience seems to bear out, is that 'God is love'. This is what the great story (the 'metanarrative') of the Bible is about – a loving God trying to restore and reconcile his world, and to draw everything into harmony with himself. It's a love story, expressed most beautifully and poignantly in a man who ended up on a cross. But in his life this man gave us the image of God as a loving Father with a love more profound and passionate, more extra-vagant and unconditional, than anything anyone had ever grasped before.

Ultimately there's only one image of God we can trust and that's the person of Jesus. God is 'the God and Father of our Lord Jesus Christ' (Romans 15.6) – and, as they say, like Father, like Son. We couldn't see God and live; we'd burn up in the glory of that vision. But here in Jesus is a human 'filter' to enable us to look at the glory and stay alive. Jesus was all of God that a human life could take without blowing a fuse. He's the closest we'll get. 'God is Christlike and in him is no un-Christlikeness at all' (Michael Ramsey).

All the other images of God suggested at the start of this chapter need to be judged in the light of this ultimate icon of God-in-Christ.

If another image or metaphor can stand alongside the image of God we see in Jesus, then it might be helpful. Otherwise it's a snare and a delusion. That's the experience and wisdom of millions of Christians through the centuries.

The heart of the matter

Human beings are addicted to fantasy and will make up pictures of God which are likely to be projections of personal need and damage. The best touchstone for evaluating any understanding of God is the person of Jesus Christ, the human face of God.

Quotes for the conversation

Prepare to meet thy God. (Evening dress optional.)

Graffito on A1

I must remember that God is not my personal secretary.

Florence Nightingale, writing in her diary

We journey because God is a traveller; we love because God is a lover; we dream because God is a dreamer.

Mike Riddell, author

If it is I who say where God will be, I will always find there a false God who in some way corresponds to me, is agreeable to me, fits in with my nature. But if it is God who says where he will be, that place is the cross of Christ.

Dietrich Bonhoeffer, theologian and martyr

Martin Buber read out to a friend a piece he'd written about faith, but the friend reacted fiercely. 'How can you bring yourself to say "God" time after time? What word of human speech is so mis-used, so defiled, so desecrated as this? All the innocent blood that has been shed for it has robbed it of its radiance; all the injustice it has been used to cover has effaced its features. When I hear the word used it sometimes seems almost blasphemous.' Buber replied, 'Yes, it is the most heavy laden of all human words. None has become so soiled, so mutilated; *and just for this reason I may not abandon it.*'

Martin Buber, German theologian

Story

Anna is a little girl with remarkable spiritual sensitivity who has a friend called Fynn who tells her story.

'Fynn, Mister God doesn't love us.' She hesitated. 'He doesn't really, you know, only people can love. I love Bossy (the cat) but Bossy don't love me. I love you, Fynn, and you love me, don't you?' I tightened my arm about her. 'You love me because you are people. I love Mister God truly, but he don't love me.'

It sounded like a death-knell. 'Damn and blast,' I thought. 'Why does this have to happen to people? Now she's lost everything.' But I was wrong. She had got both feet firmly planted on the next stepping stone.

'No,' she went on, 'no, he don't love me, not like you do, it's different, it's millions of times bigger. You see, Fynn, people can only love outside, and can only kiss outside, but Mister God can love you right inside, and Mister God can kiss you right inside, so it's different. Mister God ain't like us; we are a little bit like Mister God, but not much yet.'

From Fynn, Mister God, This Is Anna

9

Science has all the answers today

———•◆•———

What they say

- Religion used to give us the answers to life's mysteries but now science gives us all the answers we need.
- Now that we live in a scientific age, religion looks like superstition.
- Ever since Darwin, Christianity has been on the back foot. If it comes to a straight fight between science and religion, science wins every time.
- How can a modern person, brought up with even a little scientific knowledge, take a religious world-view seriously?
- Now we know about evolution, how can you believe in Adam and Eve and a time when everything was perfect?

* *

Star quote

Sir: In your dismally unctuous leading article asking for a reconciliation between science and 'theology', you remark that 'people want to know as much as possible about their origins'. I certainly hope they do, but what on earth makes you think that 'theology' has anything useful to say on the subject? . . . It is science, and science alone, that has given us this knowledge . . . What has 'theology' ever said that is of the smallest use to anybody? I have never heard any [theologian] ever say anything of the smallest use, anything that was not either platitudinously obvious or downright false . . . Even the bad achievements of scientists, the bombs and sonar-guided whaling vessels *work*! The achievements of theologians don't do anything, don't affect anything, don't achieve anything, don't even

Key issue

Many people perceive, without a clear understanding of the detail, that science has pushed religion aside and made religious belief either redundant or meaningless. Science and religion are often set up as alternatives in our understanding of reality, building on a long tradition that runs from Darwin's work on natural selection and evolution through to the modern classroom and the popular press.

What you might say

Setting science and religion against each other is an unfortunate and unnecessary mistake. People take up fundamentalist positions on both 'sides', but a more constructive approach is that of critical dialogue. Indeed, there is evidence of much more interest in this dialogue coming from scientists in recent years, and it appears there are as many Christians among scientists as among any other part of the population.

When people put science up against religion they often don't take account of the nature of different types of knowledge, and the language that goes with them. A wedding ring can be described in physical terms by its weight and density, in chemical terms by its gold composition, in historical terms by its journey from the ground in South Africa to a jeweller's shop in London, in economic terms by the hole it made in someone's bank balance, in social terms by its significance as a symbol of marriage, in personal terms by its meaning to me in my own marriage, and in spiritual terms by its significance in reminding me of God's endless love. These different languages are complementary, not competitive. We can value them all, but no one form of language should claim to be dominant or exclusive. Scientific knowledge has opened up wonderful horizons for all of us but it goes beyond its remit if it tries to pronounce on ethics, aesthetics or personal knowledge, areas that have their own integrity. Science can give us good background information but then it has to back off. For example, it can help us understand the reasons for a particular famine but it can't tell us whether to respond to the crisis. You can't get an 'ought' from an 'is'. Science and religion are complementary languages.

Another angle on this is to realize that science and religion tend to be asking different questions. Popularly it is said that science specializes in 'how' questions and religion in 'why' questions, although the distinction is not always as neat as that because there's only one reality that both are exploring. Take a kettle boiling in the kitchen. *How* is it boiling? The electricity is causing a heat exchange which is affecting the vapour pressure in the water and the water is undergoing an observable change of state. *Why* is the kettle boiling? Because I want a cup of tea. Both answers are true. The scientific answers tend to work from the bottom up with basic explanations of what is going on. The 'purpose' questions tend to work from the top down, to tackle the bigger picture. Theology deals with purpose questions.

Many scientists find themselves looking in the direction of God because of the deep intelligible order they encounter in the universe. There is an extraordinary mathematical beauty about the deep struc-tures of reality. Einstein himself said that the most incomprehensible thing about the universe is that it is comprehensible. Professor Paul Davies sees rationality in the physical regulation of the universe and wants to know where it comes from. 'Atheists claim that the laws exist without reason and that the universe is ultimately absurd. As a scientist I find this hard to accept. There must be an unchanging rational ground in which the logical ordered nature of the universe is rooted.' Or, more simply, 'if the universe is simply an accident, the odds against it con-taining any appreciable order are ludicrously small'. So it seems that the rational beauty of the universe is matched by the rational working of the human mind in such a way that they fit – the universe is intelligible.

As Professor John Polkinghorne puts it, 'The reason within and the reason without fit together because they have a common origin in the reason of the Creator, who is the ground of all that is.'

Many scientists also find themselves drawn to some concept of God by the so-called 'anthropic principle'. Why are the laws of nature exactly what they are? They seem to be so precisely fine-tuned that the smallest variation in any direction would have excluded human life. This applies to the universal forces of gravity, electromagnetism, the speed of light, nuclear forces and much more. For example, if the universe had expanded in the first few minutes after the Big Bang minutely slower than it did, the universe would have collapsed in on itself; any faster and it would have precluded the existence of life. Only the one incredibly precise critical rate allowed the existence of everything we know about the universe, including ourselves. It's the same with the emergence of carbon-based life (us!). The nuclear furnaces (stars) needed to burn with exquisite precision for billions of years; if there had been a change in the resonant energy of just 0.0001 per cent there would have been no carbon. Of this anthropic precision Sir Fred Hoyle once said, 'Nothing has shaken my atheism as much as this discovery.' And Stephen Hawking commented, 'The odds against a universe like ours emerging out of something like the Big Bang are enormous. I think there are clearly religious implications.' Of course it could be that there are a huge number of universes and we are obviously in the one in which, by chance, the conditions were right for the evolution of life. But there is no evidence of multi-universes and we are speculating beyond the reach of conventional physics into the realm of metaphysics. Now, nothing is finally proved by this astonishing fine-tuning of the physical fabric of the universe, but as Polkinghorne says, 'the anthropic principle can form part of an intellectually respectable cumulative case for belief in God'.

Another major scientific advance has had unexpected religious implications. This is the so called 'chaos' theory that has overtaken Newton's physics as our way of understanding the cosmos. We used to think that the universe was a large machine. God wound up the clockwork and it continued to tick. Chaos theory helped us to see that the universe is much more open and much more connected than we thought. The well-known butterfly effect offers the extraordinary thought that a butterfly stirring the air over Africa today will affect the weather over England in a few weeks' time. All things are connected. Science is pointing us to a much more holistic approach to life than traditional analytical methods have allowed. Ours is a world of openness and unpredictability, of relationship and connectedness, and that opens up a fruitful dialogue with religion where relationships are of the essence – particularly a relationship with God. As a result, prayer appears on the map of possibilities, as well as the unexpected events we sometimes call (rather loosely) 'miracles'.

A further remarkable discovery in chaos theory has been made recently which shows that what appears to be completely unpredictable in the way systems operate in nature does in fact have an order and a shape. These patterns are called 'strange attractors' and have been described by one scientist as having 'astonishing beauty'. Over time there is evidence of a deep order woven into what is apparently chaotic. Interesting.

All of these points must not be mistaken as offering any 'proof' about God. No such proof could ever be given. God is mystery beyond human telling, the context in which we think, not an object we can evaluate within a field of objects. Nevertheless we can see that science and religion can properly be in dialogue over the biggest questions of life. The dialogue will always be somewhat anxious; people may often overstep the mark in what they claim. But respectful complementarity should mark this dialogue. We need each other.

The heart of the matter

Science is understandably committed to proof. Religion has a different language which is complementary and more concerned with questions of purpose and value. But early Western science had clear Christian origins; Darwin in the concluding paragraphs of his

The Origin of Species wrote of 'the laws impressed on matter by the Creator'. There are signs of a growing respect in a new dialogue between science and religion but there will always be cheap shots coming from the edges where people still try and score points. And of course the idea of God that some scientists espouse is far removed from the God and Father of our Lord Jesus Christ. For Paul Davies, Fred Hoyle and others he is more like the clockmaker God who established the first principles by which the clock would work. Christianity has an altogether more majestic understanding of the awesome nature of an infinite God. This God both encompasses and inhabits the whole of creation at every point. All new advances in scientific knowledge of just how the world works are therefore yet more pointers to the magnitude of the Creator who has brought into being, and continues to sustain, such a magnificent arena for life.

Quotes for the conversation

What is it that puts fire into these equations?

Professor Stephen Hawking, mathematician

The spirit of science is naturally devout.

Albert Einstein

There's absolutely no way that any scientist will ever disprove the idea that there is a God behind all this. How could you possibly disprove that? But it just doesn't matter to me. If what we are doing is uncovering the laws of physics and that's all there is, I think it's a noble task and I'm glad to be part of it. If, on the other hand, we are uncovering laws that some deity put in place, then that's pretty exciting too. The picture without the deity is more economical, but simplicity is not always right. I think it is in this case, but who knows?

Brian Greene, author of The Elegant Universe

When Grand Unified Theories link all the forces of nature and expose the mathematical basis of creation and the elegantly simple origins of all the richness of the cosmos, mystery is not dispelled but enthroned.

Adam Ford, writer

Science can purify religion from error and superstition. Religion can purify science from idolatry and false absolutes.

Pope John Paul II

The older I get, the more I find that I am returning to those deep questions and asking 'Why?' I don't think it's enough to shrug this question aside. We do want to know why the world is as it is. Why did it come to exist 13.7 billion years ago in a Big Bang? Why are the laws of electromagnetism and gravitation as they are? Why *those* laws? What are *we* doing here? And in particular, how come we are able to *understand* the world? Why is it that we're equipped with intellects that can unpick all this wonderful cosmic order and make sense of it? It's truly astonishing.

Professor Paul Davies, cosmologist

Even when all the questions posed by science have been answered, the problems of human life will remain untouched.

Wittgenstein, philosopher

Sort of stories

Scientists are predicting that a rock three times the size of a football pitch will pass the earth on Friday 13 April 2029 and may come closer than the orbit of many telecommunications satellites. If it collided with the earth it would create an explosion with the power of 20 hydrogen bombs. But there's no cause for alarm because it will still be 22,000 miles away – rather like standing on a station platform and watching an express train go past three feet away! Science can give us that amount of specific detail.

Current scientific theories can describe the universe to a time when it was only 10 to the minus 43 seconds old – which is a shorthand way of writing 1/10,000000000000000000000000000000000000000000th of a second from the start of the universe. Science can get that close.

There are 3.1 billion letters in the human genome. An error in any one of these could spell a fatal handicap. Science has cracked this astonishing code.

Science has made all these extraordinary discoveries.
But Christians say one thing more about them:
God lives in the details.

10

The big one – suffering

What they say

- How can a good God tolerate so much suffering? Why doesn't he fix it better?
- The Boxing Day tsunami, six million Jews in the Holocaust, the massacre in Rwanda, the death of that little girl down the street – there can only be one question: why?
- If God is all-loving and all-powerful these terrible things wouldn't happen. But they do. So either he isn't all-loving or he isn't all-powerful. Which is it to be?

What the writers say

- *From* Captain Corelli's Mandolin: The doctor returned at curfew, as distressed as always when he had been obliged helplessly to watch a child groping its last blind steps along the path to death. He had walked home thinking the same thoughts that such occasions always provoked. 'Is it any wonder that I lost my faith? What are you doing up there, you idle God? Do you think I am so easily fobbed off with one or two miracles at the feast of the saint? Do you think I'm stupid? Do you think I have no eyes?' *Louis de Bernières*
- *From* The Brothers Karamazov: Tell me frankly, I appeal to you – answer me: imagine that it is you yourself who are erecting the edifice of human destiny with the aim of making men happy in the end, but to do that it is absolutely necessary and indeed quite inevitable, to torture to death only one tiny creature, the little girl who beat her breast with her little fist, and to found the edifice on her unavenged tears – would you be the architect on those conditions? Tell me and

do not lie ... It is not God that I do not accept, Alyosha. I merely most respectfully return him the ticket. *Dostoevsky*

* *

Star quote

'Sir, In the light of the seeming inability of church leaders to give any kind of acceptable theological explanation of the tsunami disaster, or of previous disasters great and small, it is perhaps little wonder that there are fewer baptisms, even fewer confirmations and dwindling congregations. After centuries of claiming to have the truth and a unique mission to explain and interpret God and his requirements to us, church leaders are suddenly found wanting. Could it be that they never really knew?'

Letter to The Times, *January 2005*

* *

Key issue

'Why does God allow suffering?' is the question that drives to the heart of faith. If belief can't cope with this challenge, people will turn sadly away, as they have done all through the centuries. But what kind of 'answer' could ever be sufficient for a mother who has lost her child? Anything would seem trite and callous. God seems to be on to a hiding to nothing.

What you might say

Accept first of all that anything said on this issue runs the risk of trampling on the holy ground of people's deepest pain. In the face of the full storm of someone's suffering, all you can do is pull on the cloak of humility and face the storm. So all that follows is just the start – of a beginning – of a first sketch – of a way of thinking – that just might – begin to help. No more than that.

Never underestimate the seriousness of the issue. Rabbi Hugo Gryn told the story of a rabbi in his synagogue in Poland on Yom Kippur. There was a man there, a tailor, who was obviously having a terrible time, muttering and shaking his fists. So when the service ended the rabbi asked him: 'My friend, what was going on there?' 'Ah,' said the tailor, 'I got into a terrible argument with God. I said to him, Look, I know I'm not perfect. There have been times when I've skipped grace, and days when I've rushed through my prayers. And yes, I have occasionally charged people for double thread when I've only used single, and sometimes I've kept a little cloth back for my children. But you, God! You take children away from their mothers. Young men die on the field of battle. Earthquakes destroy whole communities. How can you let this happen? So let me make a bargain with you. If you forgive me, I'll forgive you.' And the tailor said to the rabbi, 'Did I do wrong?' And the rabbi answered the tailor, 'My friend, you had such a strong case – why did you let God off so easily?'

But in spite of the humility we must show before anyone's experience of suffering, there are some moves we can make. First, we will do better if we adjust our way of thinking about God's working in the world from a 'top-down' approach to a 'bottom-up' approach. If we think of God acting on the world from outside and having the power to intervene when he wants and to make the occasional foray into human history, then what the hell (literally) was he doing at Auschwitz? If he could have stopped the killer of the young girl in the news, or held back the leukaemia that took my sister-in-law in a matter of days, or deflected the planes that flew into the twin towers in New York: if he could have done these things *and chose not to*, for some high-minded reason to do with our greater good, then we might be justified in bringing a charge against God of negligence, or incompetence, or even sadism.

But if we see God's interaction with his world not from above, from outside, but from beneath, from inside the created order, then we have a very different image of God. This is a God who's limited himself to working *within* the system he's created. In the very act of creating he deliberately chooses to limit his absolute power in the interests of love. When a couple 'create' a baby they do the same. They cease to have an infinite range of possible babies in their minds that they can change and manipulate; they've created a particular, discrete human being, real flesh and blood, with *this* character and not *that* one. From now on all they can do is love and suggest and persuade and argue and bribe this new human being; they can't force it to do anything, except in the most meaningless sense. Worthwhile human existence requires genuine human freedom.

It follows from this that the whole of nature, not just human beings, must be free to be its dangerous self. When the tectonic plates shifted in the Boxing Day tsunami in 2004 that was because the build-up of subterranean pressure made it inevitable. God couldn't step in and stop it because the world he's made has to be genuinely, radically free to be itself. We can't have a 'make-believe' world where reality might change if there was a danger someone might get hurt. If we fall off a cliff it's got to hurt; we can't expect to be changed into rubber so that we'll bounce. Is that a world we'd really want?

So we have a God who doesn't so much over-rule as under-rule. And in answer to the old conundrum about God either not being all-loving or not being all-powerful, we can say he is in fact both – and just *because* of the lavishness of his love he's restricted himself to working by loving persuasion. God works flat out, all the time, for the well-being of the world and its people, and amazing things happen because of that (we sometimes call them miracles), but he works from *within* his created order. That's a bigger, tougher, more risky strategy, but it's the only one that gives dignity to human beings and integrity to God.

A second move to make is to look to the centre of suffering and there to find the image of a suffering God. This bold assertion would not have been possible some centuries ago: God was seen to be above suffering or change. But the image of Christ on the cross demonstrates to millions of believers God's passionate commitment to his wounded people. Folk religion is often inclined to think at first that God causes someone's death because 'there must be a reason we don't understand'. But a more profound realization is that 'God is in this with us,' bearing the pain with us, deeply committed to our survival and the eventual reconstruction of our lives. The picture of Christ on the cross has brought strength to countless people because it speaks of a God who enters our suffering, knows it, shares it, takes it into himself, and promises never, ever, to leave us.

A third move builds on the second. It sees only limited value in looking backwards, seeking causes and explanations, and much more value in looking forwards, seeking some form of redemption and new possibility. Suffering is a great divider. Some people never recover, and understandably so, but the dark fruits of suffering can sometimes be very rich. Remarkable discoveries can be made when all the normal furniture of our lives is thrown out. The important thing about suffering then becomes not so much what *caused* it but what is our *response* to it? What will we do with this situation? And what will God do with us?

The same applies to those of us standing by. Sheila Cassidy, as medical director of a hospice, wrote this:

> I've long since given up asking the 'why' of suffering. It gets me nowhere, and I know when I'm beaten. But this I do know: more important than asking 'why?' we should get in there, and be alongside those who suffer. We must plunge in up to our necks in the icy water, the mud and the slurry, to hold up the drowning person until he's rescued or dies in our arms. If he dies, so be it, and if we die with him, so be it also. Greater love has no man than that he lay down his life for his friends.

The heart of the matter

We take off our shoes when talking about suffering because it's dark, holy ground, but again it all goes back to our picture of God. If he's a Cosmic Plumber who should 'fix' things but usually chooses not to, then we have a problem and God has a lot of questions to answer. But if he's the Divine Lover who ties one arm behind his back, so much does he love us, then we have a different relationship to explore. True love can only exist between truly free beings in a 'free' environment. God took that risk, but it meant he couldn't save us from suffering, only enter it himself, share it from the inside, and therefore change it. It's a high-risk strategy. But then love always is.

Quotes for the conversation

I cried when I was born, and every day shows why.

George Herbert, priest and poet

So there will be accidents and casualties by the million every step of the way. Yet with all the risks, its agonies and tragedies, there is no other conceivable environment in which responsive self-giving love, to say nothing of courage, compassion or self-sacrifice, could have evolved. To speak in crudely human terms, the choice before God has been this, or nothing. And, in a sense, that is the ultimate choice each one of us has to come to.

John V. Taylor, bishop and theologian

Some of you say, 'Joy is greater than sorrow,' and others say, 'Nay, sorrow is the greater.' But I say to you, they are inseparable. Together they come, and when one sits alone with you at your board, remember that the other is asleep upon your bed.

Khalil Gibran, spiritual writer

God doesn't give answers; he enters into the questions and transforms them, in the life and terrible death of Jesus.

Anon.

'There cannot be a God of love,' men say, 'because if there was, and he looked upon the world, his heart would break.' The Church points to the cross and says, 'It did break.' 'It's God who made the world,' men say. 'It's he who should bear the load.' The Church points to the cross and says, 'He did bear it.'

William Temple, one-time Archbishop of Canterbury

God lets himself be pushed out of the world on to the cross . . . only the suffering God can help.

Dietrich Bonhoeffer, theologian and martyr

We know that in everything God works for good with those who love him.

Romans 8.28

Two stories

A teacher of the Talmud who had befriended Elie Wiesel in the Nazi death camp at Auschwitz took him one night back to his own barracks where three erudite and pious rabbis decided to put God on trial. They decided in a rabbinic court of law to accuse the Almighty of allowing his children to be massacred. Over several nights evidence was presented and heard, and eventually a unanimous verdict was reached. The Lord God Almighty was found guilty of crimes against humanity. Elie Wiesel felt like crying, but nobody wept. There was a long silence. Then one of the rabbis looked up at the sky and said: 'It's time for evening prayers.' And so they all recited their evening service.

The great violinist Itzhak Perlman suffered from polio as a child and ever since had been confined to a wheelchair. On one occasion he was performing a violin concerto when one of the strings broke with an audible 'ping' in the first movement. Everyone held their breath, waiting to see what he would do. With astonishing virtuosity Perlman continued playing as if nothing had happened, playing through the finale using only the remaining three strings. The applause was tremendous, but as the noise subsided he was called on to say a few words to the audience. Sitting in his wheelchair, a living symbol of courage, he said just one sentence: 'Our job is to make music with what remains.'

Jonathan Sacks, Chief Rabbi

11

Jesus who?

What they say

- What's so special about this Jesus? A good, brave prophet, a magnificent teacher, a remarkable spiritual leader – all of that's fine. But not God for heaven's sake! Just one in a long line of brilliant moral and spiritual teachers.
- He hasn't really got a lot to do with us, has he? He lived long ago and far away and we can't really be sure of what he said or did. So we can admire him, like we can admire Socrates or Shakespeare – but he's not really relevant to our lives today.
- Didn't he marry Mary Magdalene and have several children and go to live in France? In which case, how can we trust the Bible and what Christians say about Jesus?

* *

Star quote

This Son [of God] who goes hungry, who suffers from thirst, who gets tired, who is sad, who is anxious, who is heckled and harassed, who has to put up with followers who don't get it and opponents who don't respect him – what kind of God is that? It's a god on too human a scale, that's what. There are miracles, yes, mostly of a medical nature, a few to satisfy hungry stomachs; at best a storm is tempered, water is briefly walked upon. If that is magic, it is mind magic, on the order of card tricks. Any Hindu god can do a hundred times better. This Son is a god who spent most of his time telling stories, *talking*. This Son is a god who walked, a pedestrian god with a stride like any human stride . . . ; and when He splurged on transportation, it was a

72

```
*    regular donkey. This Son is a god who died in three hours, with    *
*    moans, gasps and laments. What kind of a god is that? What is      *
*    there to inspire in this Son?                                      *
*        'Love,' said Father Martin.                                    *
*                                     Yann Martel, Life of Pi           *
*                                                                       *
* * * * * * * * * * * * * * * * * * * * * * * * * * * * * * * * * * * * *
```

Key issue

The person of Jesus has always fascinated and attracted people. The problem has come with raising him above the status of a great spiritual teacher. Particularly in today's age of relativism and scepticism about truth-claims, people are unwilling to think of Jesus as divine, although they're generally happy to acknowledge him as one of the great minds on which Western culture was built. There are other people, influenced by contemporary conspiracy theories (e.g. *The Da Vinci Code*), who believe the Church has hidden and distorted the truth about Jesus. Either way, Christian claims about the 'specialness' of Jesus are strongly contested.

What you might say

Christians make claims for the specialness of Jesus because of what he said. His teaching has guided whole civilizations for 2000 years. It's been the touchstone of the lives and thinking of millions of people, the framework of their values and moral decisions, the basis for far-reaching social reform, and the motivation for heroism and sacrificial living on a massive scale. That teaching inspired the building of hospitals and schools all over the world, as well as the abolition of slavery, the overthrow of apartheid, the collapse of communism, and the renewal of countless individual lives. It's been said that his teaching isn't so much written as *ploughed* into the history of the world. These words and ideas seem to bear the marks of the Maker, the signature of the divine playwright. They echo through history and they're etched on our culture – words about loving our neighbour, seeking the lost, taking up our cross, turning the other cheek, being the salt of the earth and the light of the world. These words speak of mourners being comforted and peacemakers being

73

children of God, of loving your enemies and seeking first the Kingdom of God, of going through the narrow gate and building your house on rock, and above all of forgiving, forgiving, forgiving. This is teaching of extraordinary beauty, translucence and indestructibility. Indeed it undergirds the modern world.

Christians make claims for the specialness of Jesus because of what he did. He lived a life of astonishing beauty and power. He strode through Galilee fascinating and challenging people, and leaving them bewildered because he slipped through all their categories. Prophet? Yes – and no. Teacher? Yes – and more. Revolutionary? No – but yes, in a way. A dynamic leader – but a servant too. Humble, certainly – but also strangely powerful. Clear and transparent – but also deeply mysterious. Friend to everyone – but somehow 'Lord' as well. He simply couldn't be categorized. The result was that what Jesus did was both wonderfully liberating and profoundly disturbing. This young prince touched people's lives with hope, but at the same time he was fiercely engaged in a battle with the powers of evil wherever he found them. Everything that distorted or enslaved human life he set himself firmly against, drawing a line of total resistance in the sand. So people were healed, backs were straightened, sight restored, leprosy cleared up, minds made whole. Wherever Jesus met evil he opposed it. The whole movement of his life, its energy and direction, was always against evil and on the side of health, freedom, forgiveness and fullness of life.

But Jesus didn't set out to be a miracle worker. It's just that when the life of God is pulsing through your veins, you can't avoid some fallout. If someone is fully in touch with God, the possibilities multiply. People were bound to be caught up in the infection of life and health that surrounded Jesus. But equally, that kind of life is a distinct threat to those who live in small, dark places. Life like that has to be put in its place, hammered on to a cross and the sap drained out of it. That too is what Jesus 'did'. So it's what Jesus did, as well as what he said, that set him apart and made people gulp and say, 'Could this be the messiah?'

The effect of Jesus on others. This was astonishing. Without a hint of megalomania he left his friends believing that they'd been walking with

God. Within a few weeks of chatting to this man about the blisters they'd developed on their feet and whose turn it was to do the washing up, these friends were making the most extravagant claims about him. He was risen from the grave, they said, ascended into heaven, back with his Father. And yet this was Jesus, the general builder from Nazareth with the big warm smile and the *penchant* for parties. Within a few years they were writing these amazing things down and giving him all sorts of exalted names and titles – image of God, true vine, living water, good shepherd, new Adam, rock of ages, morning star, bread of life, lamb of God, wisdom of God, Son of God, the beginning and the end, firstborn from the dead – and so on. These names weren't given to other prophets, 'messiahs' and spiritual teachers, so the question is, 'Why were they given to Jesus?' The effect Jesus had on his contemporaries was truly astonishing. The categories of the Jewish story of *God* seemed to fit *Jesus* like a glove.

The especially significant actions of Jesus. There were some things that Jesus did that were loaded with special significance. They seemed to carry an implicit meaning that Jesus was acting in God's place. And such actions and implicit claims have to be reckoned with. In the first place he claimed to be able to re-write Torah – the holiest Jewish teaching, given by God himself. 'You have heard it said . . . but I say to you . . .' occurs many times in the Gospels. He claimed the ability to reach into the heart of Torah and to understand the mind of God, re-applying it to the contemporary world. There's no evidence of any other rabbi ever saying anything like that. It was clearly blasphemous – unless he was right.

Alongside Jesus making implicit claims to stand in the place of God was Jesus' authoritative way of forgiving sins. There was no doubt in any Jewish mind that only God could forgive sins. But here was Jesus forgiving sins left, right and centre. A woman caught in adultery, a man paralysed by goodness-knows-what, taxmen, prostitutes, whoever was in need of it. It was completely out of order – unless it was his right.

Here's another part of the same picture. It was a common belief among the Jewish people that God's great intervention in the nation's life was on its way. The long night of their exile was coming to an end and the day of liberation was about to dawn. The Roman invaders would be sent packing and an age of peace and prosperity would arrive. This is what the apocalyptic language of the time meant. Jesus, however, in an extraordinarily bold move, applied this expectation to himself. The Kingdom was arriving in his own life and actions. He was opening the great door to the new age. That's a massive claim to make – unless it's true.

Finally we need to note the most breath-taking claim of all. Jesus believed that he had been called to go out ahead of Israel and to take the nation's place in facing the coming tribulations that would usher in the Kingdom. It was common belief that the tornado was about to strike and a time of bitter suffering was imminent, but Jesus believed that he had to go out and meet that dark Day, to take it upon himself in order to spare the people, and thus he would open up the new day awaiting not only God's chosen people but all the world of the Gentiles as well. This was the work of the cross and resurrection, but it meant an enormous imaginative leap by Jesus, and a huge claim about his relationship with God. Unless, of course, he was right.

Now these especially significant actions of Jesus, loaded with meaning, are not the same as Jesus waking up in the morning thinking he was the second person of the Trinity! It was simply that Jesus came to the conclusion that his unique destiny was to act for God in God's own way. And we can't edit that out of the story. That's the Jesus about whom we have to make up our minds. Was he deluded? The weight of Christian history says he was not.

As for the story that Jesus married Mary Magdalene, had children and went to live in France, that came from late third-century documents called *The Gospel of Philip* and *The Gospel of Mary*. These were strange Gnostic texts full of tortuous speculations written 250 years after the events they purport to describe. Typical of their genre, they convinced few people then, and no-one in the scholarly world has believed they give us any accurate information about the life of Jesus. The Gnostics had some extraordinary far-fetched stories about Jesus' childhood and ministry which were soon recognized to be telling us much more about the strange world the Gnostics lived in than about the life of Jesus himself.

The heart of the matter

It's important not to get swept along by modern attempts to relativize the significance of Jesus. The most common contemporary myth is that Jesus never believed anything as far-reaching as Christians claim, and that the Church made the facts fit its desire for power. But we need to look at the real facts because facts defuse fantasy. And the facts point to a figure of quite remarkable words and actions, about whom people were soon making ultimate claims, and who himself acted in ways that carried the implicit claim that he was acting in God's stead. This all points to the Christian claim that Jesus is the human face of God, God's self-portrait. It was a case of 'like Father, like Son'. Jesus was all that a human being could bear of God's presence without blowing a fuse. And that's what we're asked to make up our minds about. If it's true then it's the most important knowledge we can have. It means we have a window on to God himself. If it's not true then we can simply press 'delete' and have done with this illusion. But as C. S. Lewis pointed out, this is either the most important thing in the world or the most unimportant; the one thing it can't be is of only *moderate* importance.

Joke box

A mother was making pancakes for her two sons. The boys began to argue over who should get the first pancake, and their mother saw the opportunity to make a point. 'If Jesus were here,' she said, 'he would say "Let my brother have the first pancake; I can wait." ' The older boy turned to his brother and said, 'OK, you can be Jesus.'

Quotes for the conversation

I am a historian. I am not a believer. But I must confess, as a historian, this penniless preacher from Galilee is irresistibly the centre of history.

H. G. Wells

Jesus is the body language of God.

Mark Oakley, writer

I was baptised into a Roman Catholic family and grew up indoctrinated in the ways of that Church. As a lad I was very religious, much moved by the life and death of Jesus. I prayed to him every night and went to Mass every Sunday, and on all the feast days. When I come to think of it, it was all very beautiful. Now I'm ancient and don't go to church any more (the conscience still twitches a bit as a result) but I'm basically a Jesus man, still. What he said and did in his short life was pure goodness.

Spike Milligan: the last words he wrote in the introduction
to a book of religious humour

If the earth in its planetary orbit swung even fractionally nearer the sun it would become a different kind of world in which, if there was any sort of life, it would be quite a new life system. If human consciousness became even fractionally more conscious of God we would become a new humankind. This happened in Jesus. He was the new man because his entire being was in continuous response to the Father.

John V. Taylor, bishop and theologian

Story

In the following extract the lion Aslan is the Christ figure.

'Is – is he a man?' asked Lucy.

'Aslan a man!' said Mr Beaver sternly. 'Certainly not. I tell you he is the King of the wood and the son of the Emperor-beyond-the-sea. Don't you know who is the King of the Beasts? Aslan is a lion – *the* Lion, the great Lion.'

'Ooh!' said Susan, 'I'd thought he was a man. Is he – quite safe? I shall feel rather nervous about meeting a lion.' . . .

'Safe?' said Mr. Beaver . . . 'Who said anything about safe? 'Course he isn't safe. But he's good. He's the King.'

C. S. *Lewis*, The Lion, the Witch and the Wardrobe

12

What use is a dying God?

What they say

- What can the death of a first-century Galilean carpenter have to do with me?
- A religion based on a criminal execution is a funny kind of faith. It's like having an electric chair hanging round your neck.
- The cross as the central symbol of Christianity may be powerful but it's also gruesome. It doesn't project a very positive image of what this faith has to offer.
- I simply don't understand it. How can you call Good Friday 'good'?

Key issue

In a recent international poll, 88 per cent of people recognized the McDonald's logo – the big yellow M. But only 54 per cent recognized what the cross represented. The cross is becoming a marginalized symbol in Western culture and in part this is because it's seen as a symbol of violence and cruelty, which our so-called 'compassionate' society is averse to. The cross carries with it, for some people, historical associations with the Crusades, the Inquisition, colonialism, and fundamentalist Christian attitudes to other faiths. For others, the idea of a dying God is just too complex to work out.

What you might say

The cross might be a contested symbol today but it has undoubtedly inspired some of the greatest works of art the world has ever known. Paintings, music, poetry, sculpture, literature – all these have often found their noblest expression in depictions of the cross. Artists through twenty passing centuries have been profoundly moved and inspired by that enigmatic figure hanging lonely on a cross, dying such an extraordinary death. The human spirit is constantly arrested by that strange sacrifice, and finds it irresistibly rich. When the National Gallery staged the 'Seeing Salvation' exhibition in 2000 it proved to be a runaway success. When Mel Gibson made the film *The Passion of the Christ* it broke box-office records. Any choral society in the country is guaranteed a sell-out if it puts on Handel's *Messiah* or Bach's *St Matthew Passion*. Something very profound is going on here.

One of the most significant features of the Christian understanding of the cross is that it takes seriously the dark side of human experience. There's no seven-step programme to personal success, no easy ride to a trouble-free life. This faith looks unflinchingly into the abyss of dark despair and stays there, sitting it out, with all those who've tasted the sour wine of human suffering (and who hasn't?). So although we may find the cross hard to understand we instinctively know that it's saying something very important. Essentially it's stating that at the heart of Christian faith is a suffering God, not one who remains calmly unaffected by human tragedy, but one who has 'been there', and indeed is 'still there'. The shadow of the cross lies over the world's landscape and we trace its contours in events such as 9/11, the Boxing Day tsunami, the Kashmir earthquake, the Beslan school massacre – and the personal tragedies that hit us even harder. A faith that can face this kind of grief without trying to minimize it, explain it or trivialize it is a faith worth taking seriously.

There's no adequate way of explaining a mystery as profound as the cross. The point is not to explain it but to enter it. And there are a number of ways of entering this strange, dark territory. One is to think of the cross as the place where good and evil collided with cosmic force. It's important not to patronize the Passion. We mustn't reduce this epic drama to a soap opera. Here was a build-up of dark forces – the self-interest of politics, the corruption of religion, the power of the mob, the weakness of human character, the violence in the heart of humanity, self-preservation, cowardice, cruelty, jealousy – and much more. Set against all this was simply the inexhaustible love of God, incarnated in a human life. This life was, by contrast, vulnerable, undefended, forgiving and faithful. Jesus was prepared to be so misused, 'despised and rejected by men', that he would die in agony rather than become embittered and stop loving. So this life – this Jesus – proved to be completely unstoppable. He absorbed all the darkness that gathered round him, soaked it up like a sponge, and took it away to his Father. The darkness broke him, but it also broke itself.

Jesus was killed by the weight of human and structural evil. He was destroyed at the level of the flesh, but he simply couldn't stay dead. 'You can't keep a good God down.' He was raised to life on the third day – and we'll look at what that means in another chapter. But the point to note here is that this way of understanding the mystery of the cross sees it as the place where evil was defeated at its strongest point, where it took on the Son of God – and lost. The iron wall of evil and death has been breached, and we can now stream through that massive hole in the wall to join the risen Christ. The practical implications of that victory are huge. It means that in a hundred thousand places every day Christians are empowered to enter the fray against evil, hunger, poverty, prejudice, illness, despair – and know that ultimately the struggle will be worthwhile. Not immediately, perhaps, but ultimately. The victory of Jesus over evil is the core of the manifesto for Christian social action.

Another way of entering this mysterious territory is to think of the cross as the place where the sacrifice of a life of extraordinary beauty challenges men and women to a radical change of life. Here is God's life in human shape, demonstrating such courage and love, expressing so profoundly what a human life could be like, that we simply can't resist it. 'Were the whole realm of nature mine, that were an offering far too small. Love so amazing, so divine, demands my soul, my life, my all,' wrote Isaac Watts in a famous hymn. I used to stand in front of a huge cross in the middle of the nave at Canterbury cathedral on Good Friday, singing that hymn, and I knew precisely what it meant. As a bishop I remember confirming a vibrant female undergraduate who, as an agnostic, went to see *The Passion of the Christ*, and found herself with tears streaming down her face. She had to investigate a faith which could have at its heart such a figure, capable of such selfless love. When you go to the inspiring Christian community of Taizé in Burgundy, on Friday night you see hundreds of young people queuing for hours just to approach the cross on their knees and lay their forehead on that cross in devotion. Lives are changed there. There's a huge power, and for many an irresistible attraction, in this image of a suffering Christ, loving to the point of no return – and then returning.

A third way of entering the demanding territory of the cross is to think of it as the place where God was taking responsibility on himself for the mess we make of the world and of our lives. What we couldn't do for ourselves because of our human limitations, God did for us. In Jesus he, the sinless one, died for us, the sinners. The drift of this approach to the cross is caught in the well-known hymn which states, 'There was no other good enough to pay the price of sin, he only could unlock the gate of heaven and let us in.' Every so often we hear a human echo of this 'substitution'. A man in a prison camp takes the blame for stealing a tool on behalf of another person and is beaten to death. A nun in a concentration camp takes the place of a mother of young children in the queue to enter the gas chamber. A Scout leader dies when he lies across his young charges to protect them from a rock fall. A man uses his body as a human bridge for passengers trying to escape from a sinking ferry. But we have to be cautious here. It would be easy to slip into thinking that the sinless Jesus took the anger of his vengeful Father, and nothing could be further from the truth. The cross is a place of restorative justice, not retributive justice. Christians believe that 'God was in Christ, reconciling the world to himself.' He was restoring a relationship, not satisfying some abstract cosmic principle. God's action was to save us from the judgements inevitably built into the fabric of a moral universe.

So what we have above are three approaches to the impossible – understanding the mystery of the cross. (Traditionally they're called the victory, the exemplary and the substitutionary approaches.) They're just three of an infinite number of refractions of an extraordinary light falling on a prism. But they demonstrate how human minds have kept on seeking to penetrate the heart and mind of God as that most terrifying of all events took place and God the most holy Trinity went into meltdown. What kind of faith dares to explore such an idea? Only one with Christ at the centre.

The heart of the matter

The mystery of the cross isn't a conceptual puzzle to solve but a living reality to enter. Mystery in this sense isn't simply something we're too lazy to sort out, but rather a reality too rich to comprehend. At its heart is an image of a suffering God dying in some sense 'for' the world. The only way to make sense of the cross eventually is to spend time at its foot. From that position all our attempts to challenge or analyse the cross begin to look rather foolish.

Quotes for the conversation

If you strike me down, I shall become more powerful than you could ever imagine.

Obi-Wan Kenobi in Star Wars

In the French Revolution the leading figure Talleyrand was approached by a friend who was discouraged at not being able to establish a new religion. He asked Talleyrand's advice. Talleyrand said it would be very difficult, so difficult he hardly knew what to advise. 'Still,' he said after some reflection, 'there is one plan you might at least try. I recommend you be crucified and rise again on the third day.'

Anon.

The cross is the hiding place of the power of God

Martin Luther, Reformer

What use is a dying God?

We have always had a curious feeling that although we crucified Christ on a stick, he somehow managed to get hold of the right end of it.

George Bernard Shaw, playwright

If the Church is right about him, [the cross] was more discreditable still; for the man we hanged was God Almighty. So that is the outline of the official story – the tale of the time when God was the underdog and got beaten, when he submitted to the conditions he had laid down, and the men he had made broke him and killed him. This is the dogma we find so dull – the terrifying drama of which God is the victim and hero. If this is dull, then what in heaven's name is worthy to be called exciting?

Dorothy Sayers, author

As Jesus is laid in the tomb we feel the heaviness of it. The stone rolls over our hearts. So much has died. If only we could see that the dead Christ is actually an athlete, utterly still on the blocks, poised, ready to fly.

Anon.

Story

The rabbit stopped shrieking when they stooped over it, either from exhaustion, or in some last extremity of fear. Abelard gathered up the little creature in his hands. It lay for a moment breathing quickly, then in some blind recognition of the kindness that had met it at the last, the small head thrust and nestled against his arm, and it died.

It was that last confiding thrust that broke Abelard's heart. 'Thiebault,' he said, 'do you think there is a God at all? Whatever has come to me, I earned it. But what did this one do?'

'Thiebault nodded. 'I know,' he said. 'Only – I think God is in it too.'

'In it? Do you mean that it makes him suffer, the way it does us?'

Again Thiebault nodded.

'Then why doesn't he stop it?'

'I don't know,' said Thiebault. 'All this is because of us. But all the time God suffers. More than we do.'

85

Abelard looked at him, perplexed . . .

'Thiebault, do you mean Calvary?'

Thiebault shook his head. 'That was only a piece of it – the piece that we saw – in time. Like that.' He pointed to a fallen tree beside them, sawn through the middle. 'That dark ring there, it goes up and down the whole length of the tree. But you only see it where it is cut across. That is what Christ's life was; the bit of God that we saw. And we think God is like that, because Christ was like that, kind, and forgiving sins and healing people. We think God is like that for ever, because it happened once, with Christ. But not the pain. Not the agony at the last. We think that stopped.'

Abelard looked at him, the blunt nose and the wide mouth, the honest troubled eyes . . . 'Then, Thiebault,' he said slowly, 'you think that all this,' he looked down at the little quiet body in his arms, 'all the pain of the world, was Christ's cross?'

'God's cross,' said Thiebault. 'And it goes on.'

Helen Waddell, Peter Abelard

13

He did what?!

———✦✦✦———

'On the third day he rose from the dead.'

What they say

- This time you've really blown it. I'm sorry – dead men don't come back to life.
- I can accept he was a brilliant teacher. I can accept he was a top man. I can see why he might get put to death as a dangerous prophet. But I'm sorry – that's where it ends.
- The evidence for what happened is very contradictory. And there are lots of other more credible possibilities anyway: Jesus never really died, or the women went to the wrong tomb, or the disciples took the body, or the Jews or the Romans. Or the disciples needed to believe it wasn't all a waste of time. Or maybe they continued to experience Jesus' influence in their lives and the story of an empty tomb developed from there. There are loads of other possibilities.
- I might be attracted to Christianity if it was mainly about following the wonderful teachings of Jesus. But the Church insists on banging on about the resurrection, and that's where it all gets really embarrassing.
- So what difference does it make to anything – if we're honest?

****
* *
* **Star quote** *
* *
* A God made vulnerable to suffering is not today a barrier to *
* belief; if there is a God he must be one with whom humanity's *
* pain and loneliness can identify. If the man in the street or on *
* the board of management laid aside his courtesy to me and *

87

| | allowed himself to jeer, I think it would not be at my acceptance | |
| * | of the events of Good Friday. More probably it would be at my | * |

allowed himself to jeer, I think it would not be at my acceptance
of the events of Good Friday. More probably it would be at my
credulity in accepting the events of Easter. He would say that
he could not swallow the Resurrection, and he might add that
he doubted whether I could really swallow it either.

Robert Runcie, former Archbishop of Canterbury

Key issue

Dead men don't rise!

What you might say

It's an obvious presumption that dead people don't come back from the grave, but it's important not to let our presuppositions dominate our methods of thinking. A proper historical approach will want to look at the evidence and evaluate it carefully. Let's look at the main charges brought against the tradition we've received down the centuries.

The gospel accounts are so contradictory; who knows what really happened?
Of course they're different. That's what you'd expect when four different people watch the same sporting event, let alone when ordinary men are faced with an event which totally rearranges their mental furniture. But what is also striking is the unanimity of the gospel accounts on the basics – the tomb was empty, it was women who were the first witnesses, the disciples repeatedly met Jesus, his body was the same but different, the appearances came to a decisive end, the disciples were left with a job to do. The main story is crystal clear.

Jesus didn't really die on the cross; he just became unconscious but later recovered.
How, we must ask, could a man who had been flayed alive, crucified by experienced executioners, speared in the side to make sure he'd died,

and left in a tomb for two days without any medical attention, then wake up, roll away a huge tombstone by himself and emerge so fit and healthy that his closest friends could believe that he had risen from the grave and conquered death? This alternative theory is really rather desperate.

The women, confused by grief and in the half-light of dawn, went to the wrong tomb and found it empty.
There's nothing in this theory that the morning light couldn't have sorted out. When rather less confused and emotionally involved witnesses came along – people like guards, disciples, Jewish leaders, soldiers – they could soon have cleared it all up and stopped this silly rumour from spreading.

The body of Jesus had been stolen for safe keeping, maybe by the Jewish authorities or the Romans, or even the disciples.
Then why didn't the Jews or Romans come up with the body of Jesus when it all started getting out of hand? There's nothing like a dead body to quash a rumour of resurrection. As for the disciples – are they likely to have gone to martyrdom for the sake of a hoax?

The appearances of Jesus were hallucinations, wish-fulfilment. Ancient heroes of the Jewish faith were often encountered in dreams and visions – remember Daniel?
The appearances occurred to very many people (more than 500 at one time, says St Paul in 1 Corinthians 15.6), and they happened over a period of some weeks in many different places and to various groups. Mass hallucinations don't fit the facts. Moreover, those other visions of ancient heroes showed them clothed in glory, after death, and in the heavenly places, not dressed as usual, raised from death, and in the normal places. This was unique. And let's be clear: Jewish belief had no expectation of an individual resurrection; it envisaged only a final resurrection of all the faithful on the last day. Jesus' resurrection was utterly unexpected.

Stories of resurrection only developed as the disciples realized they were conscious of the continuing, empowering presence of Jesus. He had left such a strong imprint on them it felt as if they had been reborn.

This view underestimates the revolutionary effect of the resurrection event which completely transformed the lives of the disciples. They were broken and demoralized men; they were hiding away in fear and with a terrible sense of failure. But then within a few days we find them fearlessly and joyfully announcing 'Jesus is risen.' And they were unstoppable. They were harassed, arrested, beaten up, martyred, but nothing was able to keep them down. Something extraordinary had happened to them because something extraordinary had happened to Jesus.

The whole story of the resurrection was a conspiracy concocted years later by the Church to keep itself in power. The earlier, simpler stories about a human Jesus were suppressed and the divine figure we know now was inserted instead, complete with his resurrection.

This falls into the fanciful trap of most conspiracy theories – it fails to look at the evidence or at the results of 2000 years of scholarship, preferring to patch together diverse pieces of half-digested facts and ideas into a work of fiction. All that's required to deal with such wild speculations is a little knowledge of early Church history, of the difference between Christian writings and later Gnostic texts, and of how the canon of the Bible came to be formed. Oh, and of how we love to make mysterious mountains out of semi-fictitious molehills!

Having looked at the familiar charges brought against the way mainstream Christian faith has understood the resurrection event down the centuries, what shall we say positively?

The tomb was empty.
The Gospels are unanimous. The empty tomb is part of the earliest tradition and no-one at the time seems to have disputed the basic fact. The accounts have an urgent, breathless and dramatic quality with all the hallmarks of an eyewitness account (there are no Old Testament echoes, for example, unlike the accounts of the crucifixion). Moreover the witnesses to the empty tomb are women, the people in that society least likely to be believed. If you were fabricating a story the last

thing you would do is give major parts to women. There is in fact no evidence of the various accounts of the resurrection being 'fixed' to make them consistent, which would have been one of the first evidences of skulduggery. An interesting additional piece of evidence is the fact that there is no tradition of veneration at the tomb of Jesus, a common practice at the tombs of prophets or holy figures. It seems as if the first Christians were too busy meeting the risen Lord everywhere else.

The disciples met Jesus time and again after the resurrection.
Jesus appeared to his friends at the tomb, in the upper room, on an evening walk to Emmaus, by the sea in Galilee, on a mountain top, and even somewhere when 500 people saw him at the same time. St Paul points out carefully that most of those 500 are still alive. He's saying 'Ask them, if you like!' Paul's testimony goes back to within two or three years of the events themselves. We're getting very close. Again, like the empty tomb, the narratives are quite fresh and uncontrived. They have the ring of truth. It's interesting how in the first 'official' account of the resurrection in 1 Corinthians 15.3–8 the women have already been screened out and an appearance to James has come in instead. More evidence that having women as the first witnesses to the resurrection was a highly risky strategy – unless it was true!

There is obviously a mystery about the nature of Jesus' risen body. The Gospel writers are very clear that Jesus could do normal things, like eat a meal, or be touched by a doubting disciple, or prepare a barbeque on the lake shore. Equally this is a body which is quite unlike anything we've ever known. It could be present one moment and then not so the next. But that's what we would expect, surely, of a body as mysteriously renewed as this. What we have is a transformed physicality. We're beyond our normal range of understanding here but maybe we could think of it this way. Pure carbon can exist in two forms – diamond and graphite. The atoms are exactly the same but they're put together differently. Diamond is hard, colourless and crystalline, unbreakable and sparkling. Graphite is soft, flaky and slippery; it's grey and matt. If the same substance can exist in two such completely different forms, why can't Jesus in his resurrection be the same person, but in a totally different form – a transformed physicality?

The disciples were profoundly changed
We've seen this above. They were stopped in their tracks, turned round and sent off in a completely different direction. Imagine a pair of pictures 'before' and 'after' – the change from the last pages of the Gospels to the early chapters of Acts is huge, and the resurrection is the hinge. Something phenomenal happened here.

The early Church was soon exploding in size and confidence.
From that little group of frightened disciples in the upper room, through the 3000 baptized on the day of Pentecost, and then into the Gentile world, the growth of the Church was astonishing. Within 300 years Rome itself had fallen to the penniless preacher from Galilee, and now two billion people look to Jesus Christ, claiming to be his followers. That's an enormous body of people if it's all based on a mistake.

'Jesus is Lord.'
The early Church couldn't speak highly enough of him. Within a few years of his death the first Christians, including those who had known him from when he was walking around Galilee, were speaking of him as divine. This was a staggering claim to come from a Jewish background. The first Christians fell over themselves to find titles and phrases for Jesus which were exalted enough (read Philippians 2 or Colossians). Something immense and amazing had happened here.

The heart of the matter

We mustn't judge the resurrection with the stale tools of secular modernity. Exposure to the evidence leads to the conclusion that the Christian tradition is reliable – and has far-reaching implications.

So what?

The resurrection isn't a piece of interesting information to file away under 'R'. The once and future Christ is the heart of the Christian message for the world. So what does it mean?

- *Jesus is vindicated in what he said and did.* He can be trusted as the closest we'll get to the mind and heart of God.
- *Evil is disarmed and death has been overcome.* It's the day death died, and we can look beyond death with confidence.
- *God has launched his new creation on the world.* There's more to come but a new way of living has been inaugurated and we can begin to share it now.
- *Jesus is alive,* and can be encountered in a garden, a mountain top, an office, a church, our neighbour – even in ourselves.
- *The last word is life, not death,* in spite of all evidence to the contrary. And Christians are committed to both living life in all its fullness, and bringing it to others.
- *The life of the world matters hugely,* because 'matter matters' to a God of material (not just spiritual) resurrection. Politics, justice, the environment, peace issues – all may be able to anticipate God's new world which is now on its way.

Quotes for the conversation

The gospels don't explain the resurrection; the resurrection explains the gospels. Belief in the resurrection isn't an appendage to the Christian faith; it *is* the Christian faith.

John Whale, writer

[The resurrection is] a joy beyond the walls of the world, poignant as grief.

J. R. R. Tolkien, scholar and author

He burst out of that grave, propelled by resurrection – casting all before him, by the blaze of his uprising.

Veronica Popescu, poet

God is busy with his programme in the United Kingdom, from Brixton to Birmingham to Ballachulish. And that programme is a resurrection programme that does justice to the transformation God wants for his people.

Charles Elliott, academic

I handed on to you as of first importance what I in turn had received: that Christ died for our sins according to the scriptures, and that he was buried, and that he was raised on the third day in accordance with the scriptures.

St Paul

I want to know Christ and the power of his resurrection.

St Paul

Story

It was an all-age service on Easter Day and I was starting to eat a daffodil. Other preachers have done this, I said to myself as I munched through the petals. I talked in a relaxed kind of way about Easter as the congregation watched in mounting disbelief. 'He's finally lost it,' their faces said. At last I explained what had been going on. If they had gone home and said 'The vicar ate a daffodil in church today,' their families might have been entitled to dismiss the observation as the kind of thing that might be said by people who go to church too often. But if the family next door said they'd seen the same thing, and then the couple over the road, and then more and more said they'd seen it happen too, your family might have to start taking it seriously. 'And that's what happened at the resurrection on that first Easter day,' I finished triumphantly.

And then I went outside to be sick. Nobody told me you weren't supposed to eat the stalk.

Part Three

WHY GET INVOLVED?

14

The Bible – big, black and boring?

————◆◆◆————

What they say

- As well as being boring, the Bible's irrelevant. What's the dubious history of a migrant race in the Middle East over 2000 years ago got to do with us today?
- How can you trust what it says? Where's the evidence? How can you believe in Adam and Eve, Noah's Ark and people who lived for 175 years?
- Why do Christians make such a fuss over the Bible? They seem to treat it as a users' guide to the universe. 'The Bible says . . .' – as if that settles it! The Bible has been given authority way beyond its remit.
- It's very variable in quality. Some parts are exquisite and some parts are terrifyingly awful.
- Christians seem to be in such violent disagreement with each other over how to interpret the Bible, so how can the rest of us know what to think?
- Why are just these books in the Bible? Other books tell different stories but they got side-lined. Sounds like some kind of power-play.

* *

Star quotes

A teenager emailed her minister with some questions about reading the Bible:

Why am I even trying to like this? The Bible must be an extremely difficult document to read accurately. Is it worth it? I mean, it seems like everything that's presented, even in the most obvious way, has to be 'translated'. Is it really so great, and worth

97

* all that effort? If every little thing has to be read in a completely *
* different way from the way it's written, what's the point? *
* *From Brian McLaren,* More Ready Than You Realise *
*
* *A playwright claimed the inspiration for the violence in her plays* *
* *came partly from the Bible:* *
* The reading I did in my formative years was the Bible, which is *
* incredibly violent . . . full of rape, mutilation, war and pestilence. *
* Moving away from religion was my first relationship break-up. *
* *Sarah Kane, who committed suicide at twenty-seven* *

* *

Key issue

Is the Bible an important religious text but inevitably a product of its time, with all the failings that implies? Or is it a definitive script, carrying the authority of God?

What you might say

Whatever else you want to say about it, the Bible has fed the world, and changed it. The overarching story of God has made sense of the world for countless millions of people. Civilizations have taken their moral shape from its teaching. The biblical narrative has inspired some of the world's greatest art, literature, poetry and drama. For centuries no-one could be called educated unless they knew its rich text. In short, the Bible has permeated our culture and many others. Ours is the first generation to be estranged from this core script.

It's true and inevitable that the Bible is a complex document. It contains 66 books, written over a period of a thousand years by many different authors, each in a particular context and with a particular goal. The kind of literature is immensely varied too – law, history, poetry, wise sayings, prophecy, gospel, letters, apocalyptic. This is a book that has occupied the lives and skills of some of the finest minds of each generation for century after century, employing ever more sophisticated forms of scholarly criticism, historical, literary and theological.

So it's not light summer reading for the beach. On the other hand, in terms of sales, it's the ultimate blockbuster, year after year.

Discerning what kind of material we're dealing with in a particular book of the Bible is really important. For example, Genesis isn't meant to be a scientific account of God's act of creation but a truth-telling picture-story of the heart of the matter – that the world is created and sustained by God and belongs to him, no matter how much we mess up. Similarly with the Book of Revelation: it's a particular genre called apocalyptic, giving a 'cartoon-like' picture of the Last Things to sustain and encourage a persecuted Church. Because it was written over such a long period of time, the Bible is a record of a people's developing understanding of God. Descriptions of God's direct violence in parts of the Old Testament contrast with some golden threads about his mercy and endless love, all of which culminate in the person of Jesus, the ultimate icon of God. The Bible is God's book for us, but it's also our book about God, and therefore we are bound to see a developing tradition of understanding of the nature of God.

It's possible to have too 'near-sighted' a view of scripture, to get up too close and be confused by the details. We need to stand back and take in the huge sweep of its narrative. Indeed the Bible is a bit like the aftermath of a massive eruption; the important thing is the explosion and not the debris that's left lying around afterwards. That explosion was the event of Jesus – his life, death, and new life – at the centre of history, the centre of God's loving dealings with his world. The debris is all the ensuing writing based on the Jesus event and all the preparatory material which set the scene for his coming. We should undoubtedly spend time sifting through the debris but we should never forget that it's the explosion that matters.

The reason why the Bible is taken so seriously in all Christian traditions (its 'authority') is not to do with some magical process by which God dictated his words to all these writers, daring them to make a spelling mistake! Indeed the particular books now in the Bible only came to be an agreed 'canon' at the end of the fourth century when the wisdom and experience of the Church in many places led to a consensus around these 27 books of the New Testament supplementing the 39 books of the Old. Other contenders for a place in the 'canon' were either not written by an apostle or they failed to represent the faith which had been passed on from the earliest times. The normative authority of the Bible rests on two points. First, in the case of the New Testament, these are the earliest and most authentic witnesses to the life, death and resurrection of Jesus Christ, and therefore crucially important. And secondly, these scriptures witness to the authority of *God*, exercised through scripture, not to the authority of a *book* as a free-standing text. The various books of the Bible, in many different ways, tell the story of God, working out his sovereign, saving plan for the entire cosmos. The Bible therefore carries the authority of a faithful record of God's mind-bending work.

Believers need to take seriously the genuine difficulties people have with the Bible. They need not be defensive about the quality and reliability of the Bible and its effectiveness in people's lives, but they do need to understand the problems our culture has with any claims people make that give priority to a particular faith, philosophy or special book. Perhaps the best approach is to encourage people not to submit to the Bible simply as an authoritative book, but to engage in a conversation with it in the millennial chat-room of faith. Jonathan Sacks, the Chief Rabbi, says, 'The Bible isn't a book to be read and put down. It is God's invitation to join the conversation between Heaven and Earth that began at Mount Sinai and has never since ceased. God speaks in such a way as to leave space for us to reply, ask for clarification, argue the case, get involved.' This is a very Jewish way into the scriptures, but it echoes the contemporary move to value the role of the reader, not just the words of the text itself. However we put it, we need to encourage people to actually read the Bible again, and not just dismiss it as tough, passé or a mental strait-jacket.

The bottom line is that God changes lives through the Bible. Untold numbers of people have been picked up, turned around and set off on a new and hopeful path through encountering God's word to them.

They've been inspired to radical service all over the globe. They've changed the face of society over slavery, education, the Factory Acts, etc. because of what they've read in those pages. They've claimed words of reassurance when there was nothing else to hang on to. They've been encouraged to keep moving when Easter has seemed far away. In short, the Bible changes lives. It's like the Operating System in our Christian computer, the Master-tape of our faith.

How to 'read' the Bible

People are often scared of the forbidding black tome on the bookshelf, full of unfathomable words and ideas. We need to recover the idea of the Bible as a friendly companion. The simplest way into reading the Bible is to pray for illumination and then to ask three basic questions:

1 *What?* What is this passage actually about? Who's saying what to whom? Who else is around and what are they doing? Where's it happening? What's the atmosphere of the passage like? In other words, we need to be attentive to the story.

2 *Why?* Why might this passage be saying what it does? Why has it been written at all? Is there some issue going on behind the scenes? Why would the original writer want to record this and what would the original readers and listeners have taken away from it? This is a bit of imaginative detective work, and sometimes of course it would be good to have a straightforward commentary to help. (See, for example, Tom Wright's For Everyone series of New Testament guides, published by SPCK.)

3 *How?* How does this passage apply to the world I know – my own life, my church, work, community or nation? How would the wisdom of this story work out in this context, different as it is? What are the links between the Word and the world, God's eternal wisdom and my newspaper?

Behind this is another set of questions that might be a little harder and take a bit more time, but might be even more rewarding.

1 *What's the world **behind** the text?* What can we find out about the context in which this passage sits? What were the customs, politics,

economic relationships, religious rituals, etc., that are assumed in the story? We can find our answers through books and commentaries but another approach is to let our imagination reconstruct the scene and simply see, hear and feel what the place was like, how daily life might have been operating, and what begins to happen as the story unfolds.

2 *What's the world of the text?* Here it's important to be attentive to the text itself, to read it slowly and to notice what happens. Again, commentaries will help, but much detective work can be done ourselves simply by looking carefully at the kind of material it is (is it history, poetry, prophecy, instruction, parable or what?); at the structure of the passage, how it shapes up, its use of words, repeated phrases, etc.; and at echoes of other parts of scripture, and how that affects the way we understand our own passage.

3 *What's the world in front of the text?* In other words, what is our own context as we read this passage and how might the passage work out in our lives? What are the assumptions in our world that we bring to this story? How have we heard it preached and used in the life of the Church in the past and has that been right? What does it say *now*?

The heart of the matter

As we read the Bible we need to bring all of ourselves, our intellect, will, imagination and emotions, to an on-going, obedient, but challenging conversation with God through scripture. As we read it we should expect to experience the nudge of God and the call to keep exploring. And behind that conversation we can trust the veracity, quality and authority of God's special Book.

Quotes for the conversation

We present you with this book, the most valuable thing that this world affords. Here is wisdom; this is the royal law. These are the lively oracles of God.

> *Words said at a coronation when the new Sovereign*
> *is presented with a Bible*

When a man [*sic*] reads the Bible he is not merely reading a book, or indulging in a literary exercise; he is being dealt with by God.

G. K. Chesterton, essayist and novelist

The Bible, as a place of encounter and shared experience, should never be put on a pedestal. It has no need of one. Rather, it is to be befriended as the companion to faith that it is. Friends are loved, debated with, sometimes disagreed with, and are the ones we enjoy spending time with because of what we learn about ourselves, and them, in this dialogue of trustful exchange.

Mark Oakley, writer

Voltaire said that a hundred years after his death the Bible would be a museum piece. A hundred years after his death the French Bible Society set up their new headquarters in Voltaire's old home in Paris.

Anon.

Reading scripture constitutes an act of crisis. Day after day, week after week, it brings us into a world that is totally at odds with the type of world that newspaper and television serve up to us on a platter as our daily ration of data for conversation and concern. It is a world where God is active everywhere and always, where God is fiery first cause and not occasional after-thought, where God cannot be procrastinated, where everything is relative to God and God is not relative to anything. Reading scripture involves a dizzying reorientation of our culture-conditioned and job-oriented assumptions.

Eugene Peterson, author

'Read the Bible – it'll scare the hell out of you.'

On the t-shirt of a hairy biker at the Greenbelt festival

Story

A Lutheran pastor, a Norwegian, was arrested by the Gestapo in the Second World War. He was brought to the interrogation room and the Gestapo officer placed his revolver on the table between them and said: 'This is just to let you know that we're serious!' The pastor instinctively pulled out his Bible and laid it alongside the revolver. 'Why did you do that?' demanded the officer. The pastor replied: 'You laid out your weapon – so did I!'

15

What's the use of praying?

What they say

- Prayer? It's just a religious way of talking to yourself.
- It's all a bit escapist. Surely we should try and sort out our own problems rather than appeal for supernatural intervention.
- The world is as it is. How can prayer possibly change the way things are?
- If God is really God, then he should know and care about our needs anyway, without us needing to badger him about them.
- I don't like a God who seems to have favourites.

* *

Star quote

Sometimes I used to go to [school chapel] more than once a day, in that swooning, obsessive way that adolescents can have. Then almost immediately after my mother's accident, I started to walk away from it. I thought, this is crazily unfair and a betrayal of all the things that I have believed in. I lost my faith in about a week.

Andrew Motion, Poet Laureate

* *

Key issue

Prayer can seem to be either a useless activity (if God is a doubtful proposition) or an unnecessary one (if God knows what he's doing anyway). Either way, prayer seems superfluous or self-indulgent. And, in any case, it doesn't always work.

What you might say

Prayer has been one of the most natural activities for most people in most cultures through most of human history. Prayer seems to be an instinctive response to life's gifts and troubles, and it tumbles out of our mouths before we've had time to stop it. Such a universal instinct deserves our respect.

Prayer has become not just a luxury for those who've tried everything else, but a necessity for a bewildered and grumpy culture searching for stability and grace. Prayer acts as a kind of 'spirit-level', keeping us in balance when life might de-stabilize us. The pursuit of spiritual harmony may seem like another lifestyle package to consume, but underneath is a genuine spiritual void with an accompanying hunger. Isn't the experience of longing common to us all?

Prayer is not the same thing as intercession. Prayer isn't a cash-machine to produce payment on demand; it's a relationship to enjoy and nurture. Asking for God's particular activity in a situation is only one form of prayer, part of a range of activities appropriate to living in a relationship, such as giving thanks, apologizing, sharing everyday things, arguing and getting angry, being comfortably silent, and so on. Prayer isn't a cheeky way of getting something we want; it's simply being with God in a number of characteristic ways, and enjoying the privilege.

But if we stay with intercession – asking for God's particular involvement with people and places – we mustn't be seduced into thinking that science somehow makes prayer redundant. It's widely recognized now that so-called 'laws of nature' aren't iron-clad laws at all; they're simply descriptions of nature's regularities. The fabric of creation has a much more open texture than we might suppose, and so when we pray for something to change in a situation we're not throwing paper darts at an iron wall, we're stretching the fabric of creation to let God's actions show through. And when things do seem to change in some way (and there's no knowing in what way), there should be no triumphalism – nothing can be proved – just gratitude. Nor should it be thought that the regularities of nature have been interrupted; rather, we've been exposed to a deeper and fuller order of reality than the one we normally expect. It's God's will and purpose that everything should be alive to its fullest extent and its greatest capacity, and prayer is our co-operation with God in that great enterprise.

It would be easy to throw the accusation of favouritism at a God who seemed to act distinctively in one situation but to show no interest in another. If I decided not to go to work on the morning a terrorist outrage destroyed my train, can I thank God for my deliverance when scores of others died? If I'm praying for two people with cancer and one recovers while the other doesn't, was God being arbitrary? If so, he's not a God I could respect, or even believe in. So what's going on? Well, if God created a world it had to have a radical degree of independence or it would be submerged in God's own being, incapable of any kind of free response. God therefore had to limit his freedom over his creation in the interests of his love for it. So accidents can happen; tragedies occur. Within that open-textured creation God is always at full stretch, helping every part to achieve its design-potential. But there must be limits to that open-texture – intrinsic limits to what can be done. We have to come up against the 'is-ness' of things; you can't have square circles or dry rain. So one friend may be healed (it was possible in this world, and in the economy of God), while another may not be healed (it wasn't possible in the world as it is, in spite of God's fullest involvement). What we can be sure of is this: God is totally with us and on our side, and so, 'if God be for us, who can be against us?' (Romans 8.31) We are all God's favourites.

Experience would suggest that some of the most special/holy people we meet are supported by a life of prayer. Ask them their secret and they'll tell you, very shyly, that they try to spend a good deal of time with God. The greatest spiritual strength I have in my Christian life is the prayer support of a modest saint in a parish where I was vicar. She's very old now and when she goes to bed at 8.00 she doesn't sleep much, so she prays for innumerable sinners like me. Those are long nights; you can get through a lot of praying in that time, and I'm more grateful than

I can say. In my experience, people who pray a lot seem to have a gentle, encouraging spirit. They're generous of heart, unencumbered by petty concerns. They have a larger vision than the rest of us. Their lives hum with quiet holiness. We probably all know someone like this – and it's humbling.

Is there an easy way to pray?

Yes and no. No-one ever truly encountered God without being scorched in some way. To take prayer seriously is to enter uncharted territory with a map that simply says 'Here be dragons.' But the names of the dragons are the many names of Love, and encountering love is, at heart, the most natural human activity. Think then of a human relationship of love, like a close friendship. It has many expressions.

'Just getting on with it.' Much of a mature friendship is natural and unselfconscious. The friends don't bore other people with the details of their friendship. They happily get on with life with this friendship as a solid encouragement in the background. So in prayer, much of the time we simply get on with the pleasures and problems of life, with the backdrop of God's good presence as security and encouragement.

'Chatting.' Friends spend quite a lot of time in short conversations of little real consequence but considerable immediate value. 'How's the day been?' 'Shall I bring round a pizza?' 'Did you see the match last night?' So too in prayer, much of it may be in the form of brief exchanges through the day, sharing the details, praying for someone we've just met, thanking God for the sun on those trees, asking for protection for a loved one, and so on. All good material for quick, one-sentence chats.

Talking. The essence of any close friendship is good communication. Thoughts, feelings, plans and fears all need to be shared at some stage, and it needs proper time. So too with prayer. Getting closer to God needs dedicated time for thinking, reading and praying. This is where some people leave the field for an early shower!

Intimacy. Close relationships eventually graduate beyond words into the realm of silence and quiet presence. So too with God, there's a time when words fall away and silence, symbols and meditation take over. God is simply to be enjoyed (though sometimes he seems to play hide and seek, and that too is just fine!).

Key approach

Prayer is a multi-textured, multi-layered relationship with a God of infinite energy and love. If we seek to live in that relationship, to inhabit it with ease and to enjoy it, it becomes more and more a necessary and inescapable part of life.

Quotes for the conversation

Prayer is keeping company with God.

St Cyril of Alexandria

Prayer enlarges the heart until it is capable of containing God's gift of himself.

Mother Teresa of Calcutta

Prayer in some way helps to thin out the fabric of the world or opens the door of opportunity for the action of God to come through.

Rowan Williams, Archbishop of Canterbury

Learning to pray is like a child struggling with the letters of the alphabet. At first he just gets a few, then a few more, until eventually he gets confused. Little does he realize that these letters can lead him through to Tolstoy, Shakespeare, Keats, Bill Bryson and the *Times* crossword. So don't be too impatient; trust the teachers; keep going. The rewards, eventually, are huge.

Anon.

In a nationwide survey of motorists carried out by the RAC it emerged that nearly three-quarters of drivers pray in the car. Twenty-two per cent said they prayed there regularly.

News report

As a child Bishop Peter Ball had a nanny who was very devout. He met her again when she was in her eighties, and he knew she spent between 4 a.m. and 8 a.m. in prayer. She said to him, 'Bishop, can I ask a favour? I'm getting on a bit now; do you think I could have a cup of tea at six?'

Stories

Peggy Noonan was a speechwriter for Presidents Reagan and Bush Snr. In 1998 she found herself writing as a journalist about what she called the 'Terrible Big Thing' that she believed was on its way. This was before the events of 9/11 that traumatized the nation. This is some of what she wrote:

> So be good. Do good. And pray. When the Virgin Mary makes her visitations – and she's never made so many in all of recorded history as she has in this century – she says: 'Pray! Pray unceasingly!' I myself don't, but I think about it a lot and sometimes pray when I think. But you don't have to be a Roman Catholic to take this advice. Pray. Unceasingly. Take the time.

Damian McGuiness was in prison for armed robbery. He went to a chapel group to get out of his cell. He wrote:

> I went to these chapel classes for maybe two months before I got shipped out to another prison. At my last session Cossie ended by saying, 'I'm going to pray . . .' and he began to pray for us as a group. As he prayed this atmosphere just descended on the room. I watched Cossie and I thought, 'Where is he getting these words from?' His prayer was like this beautiful, eloquent throb. He was free-styling, pouring his heart out to God in a way that I didn't know. I thought in my heart, 'That's the Holy Spirit.' And in my heart I said, 'God, I want what he's got.'

That night, as I dozed off in my cell, I suddenly saw this light coming towards me that scared me awake. I realised that if it kept coming towards me it would hit me, so I woke up. I was shocked and thought, 'What was that? What was that?' Then into my mind came the words: 'Romans chapter ten, verse eight.' I didn't understand it. No-one had ever said anything like that to me before. I kept a little blue Gideon's Bible under the table in my cell, so I got out of bed and found it. I opened it randomly and – bang – it opened immediately on Romans chapter ten. I thought, 'This is weird . . .' Then I started getting goose pimples on the back of my neck. I read down a few verses . . .

Verses eight and nine said: ' "The word is near you; it is in your mouth and in your heart," that is the word of faith we are proclaiming, that if you confess with your mouth "Jesus is Lord," and believe in your heart that God raised him from the dead, you will be saved.' So I said, 'OK, Jesus is Lord.' At once I was filled with a rush from the soles of my feet, up my back and into my head. Within a short time I was dancing around my cell. I'd been touched by God. It was the most amazing experience ever.

16

Why is the Church so naff?

—•◆•—

What they say

- The Church is worn out and irrelevant in the Western world. It's hierarchical and hide-bound and shown itself to be incapable of reform.
- The Church is obsessed with the wrong things. It makes a big issue out of women being in positions of leadership, and 'active' gay people being ordained. It worries about institutional decline and about its structures. These are all signs of seriously losing the plot.
- The Church doesn't scratch where people itch. The deeper issues that people think about beyond how to get on, how to get more money and how to look after the family, are things like personal and medical ethics, the environment, safety on the streets and violence around the world. The Church doesn't seem to be talking about those things.
- Most worship is depressing, out-of-touch or banal. Compared with the quality of presentation people are used to in the media, business and entertainment, the churches' presentation of worship is amateurish.
- The Church is just irredeemably uncool.

(The term 'the Church' in this section refers to the corporate identity of the different churches together. It's used in generic form rather than to refer to any one denomination.)

Joke box

A small boy was in church with his mother, and very bored. He started to make a lot of noise. His mother turned to him and said, 'Hush, Stephen, this is the house of God.' Stephen looked around at the old pews, the cobwebs and the dim lights. 'Well,' he said, 'if I were God, I'd move.'

Star quote

I'd never been to an ordinary church service before. I have been to weddings, funerals, christenings, carol services and even harvest festivals, but I have never been to a bog-standard, nobody-there Sunday service. It all feels a long way from God. It feels sad, exhausted, defeated; this may have been God's house once, you want to tell the handful of people there, but He's clearly moved, shut up shop, gone to a place where there's more of a demand for that sort of thing. And then you look around and wonder whether the sadness isn't part of the point: those who are going to drag themselves here once a week are clearly not social church-goers, because there is nothing social happening here. This isn't a place to see and be seen. No, these people are the hardcore, the beaten and the lonely and the bereaved, and if there is a place for them in the Kingdom of Heaven, they deserve it. I just hope that it's warmer there than here, and there is more hope, and youth, and there is no need for bring-and-buy sales, and the choir of angels isn't singing elsewhere that day, but you rather fear it might be. C of E heaven is in all probability a quarter full of unhappy old ladies selling misshapen rock cakes and scratched Mantovani records. Every day of the week, for all eternity.

Nick Hornby, How to be Good

Key issue

The Church shares the problem of so many traditional institutions – people see it as part of yesterday's world, living on borrowed time. Moreover they're suspicious of it as a self-serving, top-heavy system of power and control. People are much more positive these days about networks, task groups, local responsibility, experiment, innovation, provisionality, light structures. They see the Church as out of date, out of time and out of friends. They see it as having lost its way and being in need of a serious makeover.

What you might say

Very few people love organizations. Organizations don't remember their birthdays or send them flowers. Movements of any kind start out as exciting, free-flowing, informal groups gathering around a cause, and yet as soon as they need to move beyond that first generation, or to plan for a continuing existence, they inevitably turn into organizations. That applies to a football team, the makers of baked beans or a people committed to following Jesus Christ. The question isn't whether to have an organization but what sort of organization to have. And that question seems particularly acute at this time, although there have been major crises in the Church in every Christian century.

The Church never claims perfection or moral superiority. Indeed it regularly has to face up to the need for repentance, most recently for example over incidents of child abuse by priests and complicity in anti-Semitism through the ages. What the Church claims is, rather, to be a company of sinners who recognize their need of God, a community of pilgrims following a vision of a better way brought and taught by Jesus Christ. These pilgrims are trying to live in the present by the standards of the future – from where a new kingdom will come. In the meantime, we fail!

The Church may be seen by many people as an institution but there are many other models of the Church that most Christians would much rather use. The Church is *a herald of good news* about the inexhaustible love of God; *a servant of society*, dedicated to its flourishing; *a sacrament of the presence and love of God*, demonstrating what that means; *a fellowship of pilgrims* seeking to live the way of Christ together. More modern images of the Church range from *a carnival* of motley, talented people, to *a jazz band*, improvising on a theme of holiness. 'Institution' is about the last model most believers would recognize as what they think the Church really is.

The life of the Church, and any local expression of it, is best under-stood from the inside. When you look at an old church from the out-side the windows all appear dark and forbidding. When you go inside you see those windows are full of glorious, colourful stained glass, telling stories of Jesus or pointing to the glory of God. It matters very much where you're standing. So it is with understanding what the Church is about; we need to be on the inside, part of the pilgrimage.

If the Church sits uncomfortably in contemporary society, that's prob-ably as it should be. Martin Luther King spoke of Christians needing to be 'creatively maladjusted' to the norms and values of society. The Church needs to stand in critical solidarity with any current form of social order or political culture, because all of these are provisional and imperfect – sometimes grossly so – and all are judged by the standards of the coming Kingdom of God. The Church should always be march-ing to a different drum, so when it's seduced by any particular form of government (such as in Nazi Germany or perhaps Victorian Britain) it stands in need of radical repentance. But when the Church is out-spoken in its critique of consumerism or the value being put on the life of an embryo or a terminally ill person, that uncomfortable witness is a sign of vitality, not of being out of touch. The Church will be a stick-in-the-mud if mud is the right place to be!

Starting to belong to a local church (as part of the greater, universal Church) will always take time and patience, as will joining any other body of people with passionate convictions, be it a political party or a campaign for social reform. The Church isn't interested in quick-fix answers to profound questions. Nor is it interested in providing religious entertainment in competition with celebrity chat-shows, Premiership football or the latest computer game. The Church is com-mitted to the fundamental transformation of human lives and the life of society, and so its methods will be more solid and sure, putting in foundations on which real change can take place in people's lives, visions and values. It starts with spending time with other Christians, being part of a community of particular character and quality, formed around the person and teachings of Jesus Christ. The Church uses beauty, symbols, relationships, theatre, music, art, action, prayer and parties – and much else besides, in the pursuit of this transformation. And that takes time and attention.

Sometimes we have to ask – gently – if a critic of the Church has ever actually tried it. Scoring cheap shots against the Church isn't good enough. Of course the Church is an easy hit, but it must be tried before being dismissed. And I have met some of the loveliest, most rounded and humane people in churches – and even the occasional saint.

The heart of the matter

The Church, for better or worse, is the best we've got. If Christianity is to be handed on, to offer its discoveries and riches down the years, to be more than a collection of local groups, or to contribute to the renewing of a tired world, we have to have some sort of organized Church. In reality of course, the Church is only as good and effective as its members, and we have to remember the hard advice that if ever we come across a perfect church we shouldn't join it, because we'd ruin it. (No-one is perfect.) But in God's sight the Church is the Body of Christ; it's precious and much loved and he longs to make it better. The bottom line is – we're working on it!

Quotes for the conversation

It's because the world is holy and good, but also twisted and disfigured, that certain places are set apart as redeemed areas, liberated zones, reclaimed from the forces of evil. The Church is a redeemed part of creation, not as a refuge from the unredeemed world, but rather as a foretaste of its redemption to come.

Ken Leech, theologian

Christians come together in order to meet God in the company of each other, and to meet each other in the presence of God.

David Watson, evangelist

The Church is created by the blessing of Jesus, who is himself the blessing of God. Its mission is, in endlessly varied ways, to receive, focus and distribute that blessing.

David Ford, theologian

The most loyal children of the Church are those who can only just stay inside.

Cardinal Bea

The future of the Church lies in being a community of protest rather than a society of religious self-preservation.

Bob Jeffery, former Dean of Worcester

When you were born your mother brought you here.
When you were married your partner brought you here.
When you die your friends will bring you here.
Why not try coming on your own sometimes?

From a church noticeboard

The Church is what you have left after the building has burned down.

Anon.

God invites the whole of humanity to share in his exploration of a new world. The Church is simply those members of the expedition who know the one who is leading it.

John V. Taylor, scholar and bishop

Story

A feature writer in The Big Issue *wrote of wandering round a priory in Kent and finding himself sitting in a chapel when a group of strangers came in to have a service.*

They were a pretty retro looking bunch – tank tops, Cornish pasty shoes and thick spectacles – and they were followed by a priest who proceeded to hand out prayer books. Now, under normal circumstances, I would take the piss, mercilessly. I've never been a great fan of established religion and have generally assumed that ardent practitioners are deluded, happy-clappy saddoes who make friends with God because they're too inept to do so with anyone on earth.

There was more than adequate material for a really biting satire. But there was one problem: I was deeply moved by the whole experience. No-one was more surprised than I, and no-one more determined not to be moved. I simply couldn't help it. There was a point in the service when everyone turned round to everyone else, shook hands, embraced and said 'Peace be to you.' It was brilliant. Uplifting.

No doubt you'll be thinking 'What a jerk.' I'm in complete agreement. Yet I can't escape the fact that that service was one of the most spiritually liberating experiences I've ever had. It wasn't because of the words or the actions or the dogma. It certainly wasn't because of the free wine, which was gruesome. It was, I think, because of the underlying assumption of community. The sense that in this fragmented society of ours, where the spiritual is perpetually sidelined in favour of the material: where loving thy neighbour is something you do when your neighbour's husband is out at work, that it's OK to be, well, soulful.

I found to my eternal embarrassment that tears were pouring down my face. I had the sensation of being a child again. Where once I sniggered at the faithful, I now have a sneaking suspicion they might know more than I do.

Paul Sussman

17

What's the main thing?

After all this, if the Christian faith is so reasonable and attractive, why aren't more people in our society flocking to join in? To me, it's irresistible, but maybe I've been lucky. I have to face the fact that most people in Western society are luke-warm at best about the Christian faith.

We love the remains of medieval christendom, the breathtaking cathedrals and the stunning religious art, but there isn't much sign of the young prince of Galilee striding through the world drawing the nations to his love. He seems to have been side-lined in a culture with a pick 'n' mix spirituality where religion is a leisure option, and not a very attractive one either. Western culture is dazed by its own success, and so presses on with its consumerist and utilitarian agenda, although many people would say it's in danger of outgrowing its moral and spiritual strength.

In our globalized society, where Western values are so powerful and there are enormous pressures to be sceptical about all truth-claims, what are the main things in the Christian faith that account for its remarkable persistence and growth in so many parts of the world? Remember, the Church is growing at an enormous rate all over the non-Western parts of the world. Why is this?

First, Christianity affirms the depth and mystery of every human being. There's no such thing as an 'ordinary person' in Christian faith. There's glory in everyone. We're surrounded by lives of rich colour and fascinating detail. We're unique, and uniquely valuable to God. Mother Teresa was once asked by someone whether it was really worthwhile trying to salvage a few lives when there were so many in need. But she could hardly answer the question. It was a point of view so remote from her whole way of thinking that she had difficulty in grasping it. The notion that there could be too many children was as inconceivable as suggesting that there were too many bluebells in the woods or too many stars in the sky. That's authentic Christianity. It recognizes the value and the mystery of every living being. In a world where people are often made to feel disposable, this is a precious affirmation.

A second reason for the endurance of the Christian faith is its realism about the dark side of life, the reality of evil, the fatal flaw, the fracture that runs through everything. It emerges *here* in a political tyrant, *there* in a famine, *here* in my own selfishness, *there* in a friend's cancer. The glory and the terror of life are both true, and Christianity doesn't attempt to explain away the lumpy bits in human experience. *The Times* once had a lengthy correspondence on the subject of what's wrong with the world, but the final letter came from the author G. K. Chesterton who wrote: 'Dear Sir, What's wrong with the world? I am. Yours faithfully . . .' It's the way we are. It's the way the world is. But all of it, the darkness as well as the light, is seen by the Christian as being within the embrace of God, and he never gives up. For further details, see the cross.

A third reason for the persistence of the Christian faith is its brilliant model of God. It's called the Trinity. We know God in creation (the Father); God in history (the Son); and God in us (the Holy Spirit). God above, God beside, God within. The Trinity is a community of love, and this wonderfully rich and dynamic model means we have a God for whom relationships are crucial. Other faiths have great strengths from which we can learn, but Christianity has this to offer: an understanding of God the Father, known through the Son and experienced through the Holy Spirit – simple and complex, accessible and subtle, God beyond our imagination and yet God-with-us. Brilliant.

The fourth reason why the Christian faith is so durable is that at its heart is love. When all other words have stumbled and fallen over, the word which best describes God in Christian understanding is that he is Love. Love in its pure, uncut, undiluted form. God gives himself to us abundantly and recklessly in what we call grace, which is love reaching out towards us. And our response to this gift in the Christian scheme of things is also one of grace. What we do for others shouldn't be done out of duty or from a moral code, but rather out of generosity and moral inventiveness. A clergyman came back to the theological college I attended where he'd been a real problem to the staff. The students asked him what it was like, out there in ministry. 'It's all grace,' he said, and meant it. That's the authentic Christian voice again. Grace, generosity, forgiveness, love. Because God *is* love.

Another part of the distinctiveness of Christianity is that it puts the poor centre-stage. It re-visions the world with the disadvantaged at the centre. There aren't many votes in that, but it's critical for people of faith. 'Whatever you did for the least of these brothers and sisters of mine, you did for me,' said Jesus. Jesus lives in the poor, and so if we ask where God is in the desperate situations we see on television, the answer is that he's precisely *there*; the man of sorrows is ahead of us, in the suffering of his people. Here is no nice, tidy, shiny God, vacuum-packed for cleanliness, untouched by dirt and death. Here is a *suffering* God, and as the martyred theologian Bonhoeffer said, only a *suffering* God will do. How we treat the poor is central to Christianity. Hence the Christian voice is always raised over such things as issues of debt, proper aid and fair trade.

If we take that commitment one stage further we see that central to the Christian faith is the belief that the Church is announcing and celebrating the Kingdom of God, and that kingdom is nothing less than a healed creation. In such a new world every part is reconciled to every other part, and every human group flourishes in its own way. People enjoy and respect one another and don't fly planes into tall buildings or invade each other's countries or rape the environment or grab all the wealth they can get for themselves. There's nothing mean or parochial about such a programme. It reflects the fact that God loved his world so much that he came to it in the person of Jesus to lead it back to joy.

There's one other point about the persistence of Christianity. This faith offers a truly radical reassessment of life and death, and power and

121

weakness, and that reassessment comes about through the cross and resurrection of Jesus. Nothing in religion prepares us for the beauty and terror of a crucified God. Nothing in human experience leads us to expect the extraordinary shattering of death that we see in the Easter tomb. The cross stands in solemn warning over against all human pride and arrogance. The resurrection stands as a crazy promise in the midst of all disaster. The resurrection is a drama we can never domesticate for prime-time viewing, a tiger we can never tame.

If Christians are asked what's the main thing in their faith, hopefully some of these seven elements will emerge in one form or another. They form a powerful statement of the distinctive elements of a faith which has irrevocably shaped the world and transformed the lives of countless individuals.

Quotes for the conversation

I am not what I ought to be; I am not what I wish to be; I am not what I hope to be; but, by the grace of God, I am not what I was.

John Newton, hymn-writer, former slave trader

Would you know your Lord's meaning in this? Learn it well. Love was his meaning. Who showed it you? Love. What did he show you? Love. Why did he show you? For love. Hold fast to this and you shall learn and know more about love, but you shall never know nor learn about anything *except* love for ever.

Julian of Norwich, medieval mystic

According to the theory of aerodynamics, and as may be readily demonstrated by means of a wind tunnel, the bumble bee is unable to fly. This is because the size, weight and shape of his body in relation to his total wing span, makes flight impossible. But the bumble bee, being ignorant of these scientific facts and possessing considerable determination, does fly – and makes a little honey too.

Francis Clifford, The Naked Runner

What's the main thing?

Abbot Lot went to see Abbot Joseph in the desert and he said, 'Father, as I am able, I keep my little rule and my little fast and my prayer and meditation and contemplative silence; and as I'm able I strive to cleanse my heart of thoughts. Now, what more should I do?' Abbot Joseph rose up in reply and stretched out his hands to heaven, and his fingers became like ten lamps of fire. He said: 'Why not be totally changed into fire?'

Anon.

I have come that they may have life, and have it abundantly.

Jesus

Story

A man went to a wedding in Canterbury cathedral and later sent an email to the priest who had taken the service:

I joined my wife at the Eucharist on Sunday morning, after the wedding. I went out of curiosity to be in that magnificent building one more time. I admit that I haven't been to church for as long as I can remember. I didn't join my wife in communion; I wanted to, but I didn't understand why. Was it just the romance of the occasion? I felt the time spent in reflection was more important. We left the cathedral and I have to admit I sobbed. There are many things that really came to the surface with a surge. I needed to talk to my wife and express how I truly felt. I don't know whether I've found religion; it's too early to say for I'm a cynical devil at the best of times, but I thought you would appreciate the knowledge that something magical happened to me last weekend.

How to use the chapters in a home group

With some imagination these chapters could be used in several ways in a small group. What follows is just one method, which would need to be adapted to suit the session and the character of the group. I suggest, however, that a possible format is based on these phases:

Stories: encounters in the past week
Starter: identifying the problem
Sharpener: sharpening up the problem
Suggestions: tackling the issues
Sayings and stories: further help
Spirit: prayer and reflection

This is what I mean:

Stories

Share any experiences of the past week when group members have been 'on the spot' with regard to their faith or when they have come across people (outside church circles) discussing issues which relate to faith. By this means a picture will build up, over time, of how many different ways issues of faith come up in everyday life. The group members will probably gradually gain encouragement from each other and be able to enter into discussion in those situations.

Starter

Look at 'What they say' and 'Star quote' and see where and when those particular issues have hit home for members of the group. It could have been a discussion they'd once been in, an event at work, a news item, something a friend once said, a problem one of the group had had with this subject. The group is gaining ownership of the issue in its own terms.

Sharpener

1 See which of the statements under 'What they say', or from what members have said so far, represents the major issue for this group. How precisely does the issue bite?
2 Two members of the group might volunteer to play devil's advocate and put the issue as sharply as they like, inviting a first response from the rest of the group. This would lead into the next phase of the session.

Suggestions

Look at the section 'What you might say' and discuss the merits of the different approaches to the issue under consideration. Are they convincing? What are the weaknesses? How could they be improved? How would you put it? What illustrations could you give? Try to imagine specific situations and the response of particular people in order to focus the discussion.

It would help if someone has done some more preparation for this session and could point to biblical material, further reading (have the books there if you can), or the vicar's phone number!

Sayings and stories

Look at the material 'Quotes for the conversation' and 'Story' and discuss whether any of it adds anything to what has already been discussed. Allow reactions to the material, positive, negative and questioning.

Spirit

End with prayer and reflection. This could include:

- A time of silence.
- Gathering up some of the key things people have said and offering them back to God in meditative prayer.
- Remembering some of the people and situations that have been mentioned and praying for them out loud or in silence.
- A Bible reading, relevant to the topic.
- A piece of music for reflection.

- The lighting of candles for particular people in need, possibly related to the topic.
- The use of a small prayer tree to pray for people and places.

There are doubtless many other ways of using the material that an experienced small group leader could devise or adapt. The hope would be that Christians would become more confident in 'giving an answer for the hope that is in them'.

If you want to read more

General background

Joan Bakewell (ed.), *Belief* (Duckworth Overlook, 2005).
Conversations with leading thinkers demonstrating the huge variety of ways that intelligent people address the big questions.

Michael Paul Gallagher, *Dive Deeper: The human poetry of faith* (DLT, 2001).
A surprising and imaginative look at 'the issues underlying the issues' that make it difficult for many people to believe.

Richard Harries, *God Outside the Box* (SPCK, 2002).
Takes seriously the questions and objections to Christian belief that come from thoughtful people in contemporary society. Doesn't duck the hard ones.

Bel Mooney, *Devout Sceptics* (Hodder and Stoughton, 2003).
Conversations with a range of distinguished people about profound issues of faith and doubt. Taken from the BBC radio series of the same name.

Post-modern context

John Drane, *Cultural Change and Biblical Faith* (Paternoster, 2000).
The implications for Christians and for the Church of the major changes now transforming Western culture.

Gerard Kelly, *Get a Grip on the Future Without Losing Your Hold on the Past* (Monarch, 1999).
A lively analysis of contemporary culture and its future directions.

Mike Riddell, *Deep Stuff* (Lion, 1999).
An imaginative narrative approach to the social context in which we now live and how big questions arise.

Theology and apologetics

Peter Cotterell, *Mission and Meaninglessness* (SPCK, 1990).
A thorough biblical exploration of the meaning of mission.

Alister McGrath, *Bridgebuilding: Effective Christian apologetics* (IVP, 1992).
A valuable analysis of contemporary world-views and how to relate to them as Christians.

Vincent O'Donovan, *Christianity Rediscovered* (SCM Press, 1978).
A classic on how to engage with a culture other than our own.

Andrew Walker (ed.), *Different Gospels: Christian orthodoxy and modern theologies* (SPCK, 1993).
Valuable chapters on the New Testament, miracles, the resurrection, pluralism and more.

God, the universe and everything

David Atkinson, *God So Loved the World* (SPCK, 1999).
Believing in God in the context of science, psychology, and ethics in the modern world.

Alister McGrath, *Dawkins' God* (Blackwell Publishing, 2005).
A lucid and thorough-going response to Richard Dawkins' atheism.

John Polkinghorne, *Quarks, Chaos and Christianity* (SPCK, 1994).
A clear and lively account of belief in God, prayer, miracle, etc. by a former Cambridge Professor of Mathematical Physics. One of many valuable books by the author.

Keith Ward, *God, Chance and Necessity* (Oneworld Publications, 1996).
A refutation of scientific atheism from a former Regius Professor at Oxford.

David Wilkinson, *God, Time and Stephen Hawking* (Monarch, 2001). Describes the implications of modern cosmology for belief in a Creator. Written by a minister with a PhD in astrophysics.

Jesus, cross and resurrection

David Day, *Pearl beyond Price* (HarperCollins, 2001). An immensely readable book on the attractiveness and relevance of Jesus.

James D. G. Dunn, *The Evidence for Jesus* (SCM Press, 1985). An accessible introduction to the world of scholarship about Jesus from a former Professor of Divinity at Durham.

John Pritchard, *Living Easter through the Year* (SPCK, 2005). Easy reading on the facts and significance of the resurrection.

John V. Taylor, *The Christlike God* (SCM Press, 1992). A masterly account of the nature and impact of Jesus with particularly moving chapters on the significance of the cross.

N. T. Wright, *Jesus and the Victory of God* (SPCK, 1996).

N. T. Wright, *The Resurrection of the Son of God* (SPCK, 2003). Two huge and impressive volumes on historical and theological questions surrounding the life, death and resurrection of Jesus. Very readable but they take a lot of time!

The Bible

Pat and David Alexander (eds.), *The New Lion Handbook to the Bible* (Lion, 1999).

John Bowker (ed.), *The Complete Bible Handbook* (Dorling Kindersley, 1998). Comprehensive resource books, lavishly illustrated.

Tom Wright, *Scripture and the Authority of God* (SPCK, 2005). A leading biblical scholar on the proper meaning of the authority of scripture.

Spirituality

John Drane, *Do Christians Know How To Be Spiritual?* (DLT, 2005).
Connecting with spiritual seekers in contemporary Britain.

Gordon Mursell, *English Spirituality* (2 vols.) (SPCK, 2001).
Wonderfully comprehensive account of the riches of the English spiritual tradition.

Gordon Mursell (ed.), *The Story of Christian Spirituality* (Lion, 2001).
The simple version, with pictures!

Geoffrey Rowell, Kenneth Stevenson, Rowan Williams (eds.), *Love's Redeeming Work: The Anglican quest for holiness* (Oxford, 2001).
An impressive collection of writings from every era.

Finding faith

Steven Croft et al., *Evangelism in a Spiritual Age* (Church House Publishing, 2005).
Combines research, cultural analysis, theology and action.

Jeffery John (ed.), *Living Evangelism* (DLT, 1996).
Sharing faith from an Anglican Catholic perspective.

Bob Mayo et al., *Ambiguous Evangelism* (SPCK, 2004).
Communicating faith in a culture that doesn't know the Christian story.

Brian McLaren, *Finding Faith* (Zondervan Publishing House, 1999).

Brain McLaren, *More Ready than You Realize* (Zondervan Publishing House, 2002).
A book of arguments and a book of narrative from an American who has thought deeply and practised wisely.

John Saxbee, *Liberal Evangelism* (SPCK, 1994).
Demonstrates the contribution that liberal approaches to faith can make to sharing the Good News in this generation.

John V. Taylor, *A Matter of Life and Death* (SCM Press, 1986).
A gem about coming alive to the gospel.

The Church today and tomorrow

Council for Mission and Public Affairs, *Mission-shaped Church* (Church House Publishing, 2004).
An important report on church planting and fresh expressions of church for the future.

John Drane, *The McDonaldization of the Church* (DLT, 2000).
Maintaining credibility in a spiritual age. Hard and important messages for the Church.

Eddie Gibbs and Ian Coffey, *Church Next: Quantum changes in Christian ministry* (IVP, 2001).
Examines some of the major issues the Church must face urgently.

Michael Moynagh, *emergingchurch.intro* (Monarch, 2004).
Fresh expressions of church, why they matter, principles and examples.

Graham Tomlin, *The Provocative Church* (SPCK, 2002).
A serious theology of evangelism through the quality of life of the local church.

Pete Ward, *Liquid Church* (Paternoster, 2002).
A bold vision of what might be needed to be God's people in a 'liquid' culture.

The Society for Promoting Christian Knowledge (SPCK) was
founded in 1698. Its mission statement is:

To promote Christian knowledge by

- **Communicating the Christian faith in its
  rich diversity;**
- **Helping people to understand the Christian faith
  and to develop their personal faith; and**
- **Equipping Christians for mission and ministry.**

SPCK Worldwide serves the Church through Christian
literature and communication projects in over 100 countries, and
provides books for those training for ministry in many parts of
the developing world. This worldwide service depends upon the
generosity of others and all gifts are spent wholly on ministry
programmes, without deductions.

SPCK Bookshops support the life of the Christian community
by making available a full range of Christian literature and other
resources, providing support for those training for ministry, and
assisting bookstalls and book agents throughout the UK.

SPCK Publishing produces Christian books and resources,
covering a wide range of inspirational, pastoral, practical and
academic subjects. Authors are drawn from many different
Christian traditions, and publications aim to meet the needs of a
wide variety of readers in the UK and throughout the world.

The Society does not necessarily endorse the individual views
contained in its publications, but hopes they stimulate readers to
think about and further develop their Christian faith.

For further information about the Society, visit our website at
www.spck.org.uk or write to:
SPCK, 36 Causton Street,
London SW1P 4ST, United Kingdom.